Conversation Club:

Teaching Children with Autism Spectrum Disorder and Other Social Cognition Challenges to Engage in Successful Conversations with Peers

Instructor Manual

*Lynn Cannon, Jonna Clark,
Courtney Kornblum, Eve Müller,
Michal Powers*

Character illustrations by Bobby Whalen

Purchasers of *Conversation Club* are granted permission to print materials from the *Instructor Manual* and *Storybooks* at www.aapcpublishing.net/ccdw. None of the handouts may be reproduced to generate revenue for any program or individual. Unauthorized use beyond this privilege is prosecutable under federal law.

6448 Vista Drive
Shawnee, KS 66218
www.aapcpublishing.net

© 2016 The Ivymount Corporation

All rights reserved. With the exception of the Appendix, which may be downloaded at www.aapcpublishing.net/ccdw, no part of the material protected by this copyright notice may be reproduced or used in any form or by any means, electronic or mechanical, including photocopying, recording, or by any information storage and retrieval system, without the prior written permission of the copyright owner.

Purchasers of *Conversation Club* are granted permission to print materials from the *Instructor Manual* and *Storybooks* at www.aapcpublishing.net/ccdw. None of the handouts may be reproduced to generate revenue for any program or individual. Unauthorized use beyond this privilege is prosecutable under federal law.

All illustrations and characters have been created by the authors and illustrators. Use of the *Conversation Club* characters or reproduction of the artwork and characters is strictly prohibited.

Ivymount Corporation
www.ivymount.org
11614 Seven Locks Road Rockville, MD 20814
www.ivymount.org

Publisher's Cataloging-in-Publication

Names:	Cannon, Lynn (Lynn M.), author. | Clark, Jonna, author. | Kornblum, Courtney, author. | Müller, Eve, author. | Powers, Michal, author. | Whalen, Bobby, illustrator.
Title:	Conversation club : teaching children with autism spectrum disorder and other social cognition challenges to engage in successful conversations with peers : instructor manual / Lynn Cannon, Jonna Clark, Courtney Kornblum, Eve Müller, Michal Powers ; character illustrations by Bobby Whalen.
Description:	Lenexa, KS : AAPC Publishing, [2018] | Includes bibliographical references.
Identifiers:	ISBN: 978-1-942197-35-5 LCCN: 2018933848
Subjects:	LCSH: Autism spectrum disorders--Patients--Language--Study and teaching. | Autism spectrum disorders--Patients--Means of communication--Study and teaching. | Conversation --Study and teaching. | Communicative competence--Study and teaching. | Interpersonal communication in children--Study and teaching. | Social skills in children--Study and teaching. | Autism spectrum disorders--Patients--Life skills guides--Study and teaching. | Teachers of children with disabilities--Handbooks, manuals, etc.
Classification:	LCC: LC4717.8 .C36 2018 | DDC: 371.94--dc23

Artwork: Shutterstock.com and Vecteezy.com
This book is designed in ITC Stone Serif and ITC Stone Sans.
Printed in the United States of America.

Acknowledgments

The authors would like to thank the following people who contributed significantly to this book:

All the students who eagerly learned about conversation using earlier versions of Conversation Club, and helped us figure out what worked and what didn't, and to their families for supporting this process.

Katherine Driggs, classroom teacher and key member of the team that first developed and tested Conversation Club.

Christina Beachley, Laraine Brady, Brenna Haffner, and their assistant teachers for testing Conversation Club with the students in their classrooms and providing invaluable feedback along the way.

All the paraprofessionals who helped implement Conversation Club.

Susan Lee, who worked closely with Bobby Whalen, our illustrator, to create a wonderful cast of Conversation Club characters.

Amy Baker and Molly Whalen for doing such an amazing job with initial layout, editing, and production.

Lee Oppenheim and Jan Wintrol for providing administrative support and helping us figure out the intricacies of the publishing process.

Dedication

Dedicated to all the Ivymount students

who inspired this book from beginning to end.

Table of Contents

Introduction 1

Unit 1: Welcome to the *Conversation Club* 13

Unit 2: Selecting and Staying on Topic 35

Unit 3: Keeping the Conversation Going 57

Unit 4: Using Our Eyes and Ears to Think about Our Conversation Partner 77

Unit 5: Conversation Repair 93

Unit 6: Remembering What Our Conversation Partner Says 119

Unit 7: Expanding the Depth and Breadth of Conversation 135

Unit 8: Bringing It All Together 153

References 171

Purchasers of *Conversation Club* are granted permission to print materials from the
Instructor Manual and *Storybooks* at www.aapcpublishing.net/ccdw.
None of the handouts may be reproduced to generate revenue for any program or individual.
Unauthorized use beyond this privilege is prosecutable under federal law.

Introduction

What is *Conversation Club*?

Conversation Club is the first curriculum of its kind to provide a comprehensive instructional framework for teaching both the "how" and "why" of conversation. It is designed to target the needs of elementary-aged children with high-functioning autism (HFA) and other social cognition challenges. The *Conversation Club* will help instructors guide children through the rudiments of conversation by introducing them to a clubhouse filled with a kid-friendly cast of club members, including *Friendly Freddy* (the President of the Club); the twins, *Looking Louie* and *Listening Lisa*; *Fix It Farrah*; *Good Memory Maria*; *New Words Nate*; and the club mascot, *Paco the Parrot*. Club meetings are specially designed to facilitate thinking about the social significance underlying each conversation skill. Conversation goal areas include conversation initiation and topic selection, topic maintenance, perspective taking and social motivation, environmental awareness and body readiness, active listening behaviors, gaining attention behaviors, and conversation repair.

Why this Intervention Is Necessary

Healthy social and emotional development, and especially positive peer relationships, have been shown to have a significant impact on students' academic success (Payton, Weissberg, Durlak, et al., 2008; Zins, Bloodworth, Weissberg, et al. 2007). Conversation is an important means of building and maintaining friendships with peers, but for most individuals with HFA, the ability to carry on a conversation remains frustratingly out of reach. For example, children with HFA experience difficulty establishing joint attention, initiating conversation, selecting topics, making relevant contributions, taking turns, and using eye contact and other nonverbal means to indicate engagement (Burack, Charman, Yirmiya, & Zelazo, 2001; Wetherby & Prizant, 2000). Many also display "unexpected" conversational behaviors, such as immediate or delayed echolalia, which pose a challenge to conversational continuity and relevance (Winner, 2007). Why is this so difficult for children with HFA? Meaningful conversation requires the ability to quickly and accurately process a great many rapidly changing social stimuli (both verbal and nonverbal), and respond flexibly and appropriately to the conversational context. Conversational competence further requires awareness of and sensitivity to one's conversation partner.

This is all part of what is known as "social cognition," or the mental processes we use to make sense of our social world (Fiske & Taylor, 2013). As a result of brain-based differences, individuals with HFA experience significant social cognitive impairments (Striano & Reid, 2008). These include challenges related to perspective taking – or what Baron-Cohen and colleagues describe as an impaired "theory of mind," or inability to attribute mental states (e.g., thoughts, beliefs, and desires) to oneself and to others, and to understand that others' mental states may be different from our own (Baron-Cohen, Leslie, & Frith, 1985). Although many children with HFA are able to pass basic theory of mind tests, most continue to struggle with inferring peers' thoughts and feelings based on verbal and non-verbal contextual clues (Baron-Cohen, Wheelwright, Hill, Raste, & Plumb, 2001). Klin and colleagues (2003) further argue that children with autism, including those with HFA, lack a natural ability to identify and focus on salient social stimuli, which makes it incredibly difficult for them to respond to the quick-fire, moment-by-moment unfolding of most social interactions. Further, children with HFA appear to process memories in ways that differ significantly from their typically developing peers, which makes it difficult for them to access detailed information about themselves and others (Goddard, Howlin, Dritschel, & Patel, 2007; Tanweer, Rathbone, & Souchay, 2010). This is yet another way in which brain-based differences make it harder for children with HFA to engage in conversation that is responsive to their partners' interests, and takes into consideration information that their partners may have shared with them at an earlier time. The *Conversation Club* will help instructors systematically address each of these social cognitive challenges to successful conversation in a fun and unique way.

How the Conversation Club Builds on Existing Work in the Field

The *Conversation Club* curriculum uses an adapted version of the Teaching Interaction Procedure (TIP) framework. TIP offers a pedagogical model for instruction that includes providing a *rationale* for why learning a skill is important, breaking each skill into its component parts, demonstrating/modeling the skill, and providing opportunities for students to practice the skill with scaffolded support, feedback, and reinforcement (Dotson, Leaf, Sheldon, & Sherman, 2010; Leaf, Taubman, Bloomfield, Palos-Rafuse, Leaf, McEachin, & Oppenheim, 2009; Leaf et al., 2010). Several recent studies suggest that this comprehensive pedagogical approach has been particularly effective in teaching social skills to students with ASD and other social cognition challenges (Dotson et al., 2010; Leaf et al., 2010; Leaf et al., 2009). The *Conversation Club* is also inspired by Madrigal and Winner's social skills curriculum (2009), which stresses the importance of teaching "social thinking" (the ability to grasp the underlying social significance of specific skills) and ties social thinking concepts to highly motivating super heroes/cartoon characters.

How Instructors and Students Helped Us Write This Manual

Building on the work of Leaf, Madrigal, Winner, and others, we developed the manual and materials for *Conversation Club* using an iterative process that included ongoing testing of the curriculum and feedback from instructors and students. We used a bottom-up approach: Instead of developing the intervention in the lab and *then* adapting it to actual school settings, we started with the effective techniques that instructors were already using to build their students' conversation skills.

Our research and development team included Ivymount School's program evaluator, the social learning coordinator, our elementary school speech language pathologist, occupational therapist, and mental health provider. The development and feedback process then proceeded through a series of stages built on the participatory approach, which included: (a) observations of expert teachers and related service providers to identify effective instructional strategies; (b) several small trials of *Conversation Club,* followed by modification of the curriculum to address student and instructor outcomes; and (c) interviews with key stakeholders to establish social validity of the curriculum. This participatory process defined the curriculum's structure, delivery, and teaching methods, and ultimately helped us streamline the lessons. The resulting manual describes a curriculum designed for regular use (e.g., 3-4 times per week) in a school-based setting.

Others who helped make this manual a reality included Bobby Whalen, an Ivymount high school student who created all of the Conversation Club characters and other illustrations; and Amy Baker and Molly Whalen, who were responsible for the initial design, layout, and copy editing of the manual and social stories. We also want to recognize the incredible teachers, Katherine Driggs, Laraine Brady, and Brenna

Haffner; and therapist, Christie Beachley, who have helped bring this curriculum to life at Ivymount and provided us invaluable feedback throughout the process.

Does *Conversation Club* Work?

Prior to creating the *Conversation Club* curriculum, Ivymount instructors reported that students were making minimal or no progress in their ability to converse with one another. Students displayed little awareness of or regard for others in their environment, rarely initiated conversations, and required significant adult prompting to select a topic, engage in conversation with one another, and maintain interest in the conversation. Based on observations of students, however, instructors were confident that students did in fact want to engage with one another, but simply lacked the skills to do so. The *Conversation Club* was created to address these deficits.

After several years of using the *Conversation Club* curriculum with our students, we were confident that the program offered an effective means of engaging participants' attention and teaching them to be more successful conversationalists – both during instruction and in non-instructional contexts. The following section summarizes results from our two-year pilot study of seven club members, all of whom ranged from 7-10 years of age and were diagnosed with HFA and other social cognition deficits. Our findings were recently published in *Language, Speech and Hearing Services in Schools* (Müller, Cannon, Kornblum, Clark, & Powers, 2016).

We collected data by videotaping pairs of participants while they sat together and ate lunch; each recorded session was for a period of approximately 20 minutes. We videotaped each participant one or two times to provide a baseline, and three times at the end of the academic year.

Key findings from our pilot study include the following:

- **Peer-Directed Interactions** – Club members barely interacted with their peers at baseline (an average of 7.2 peer-directed interactions per 20-minute period), but by the end of the program, their conversations with peers were both longer and more frequent (averaging 68.8 peer-directed interactions per 20-minute period).

- **Questions** – Club members' conversations averaged only 2.25 peer-directed questions at baseline, but by the end of the program, conversations averaged 19.1 peer-directed questions.

- **WH Queries** – Club members' conversations averaged 0.9 peer-directed WH queries at baseline, but by the end of the program, conversations averaged 8.8 peer-directed queries. WH queries are questions that ask who, what, when, where, or why.

- **Attention-Gaining Strategies** – Club members' conversation averaged 1.9 peer-directed attention-gaining strategies at baseline, but by the end of the program, conversations averaged 6.5 peer-directed attention-gaining strategies.

- **Conversation Repair** – Club members' conversations averaged 0.1 attempts at peer-directed conversation repair at baseline, but by the end of the program, conversations averaged 2.8 attempts at peer-directed conversation repair.

These findings from our pilot study suggest that the *Conversation Club* offers an effective means of improving club members' conversation skills. We believe that club members' success was positively influenced by the curriculum's attention, not only to teaching the "how" of conversation, but also to making the "why" of conversation explicitly clear.

Selecting Club Members

Conversation Club is ideal for elementary school students aged 6–11 with HFA and other social cognition challenges. Because meaningful conversation is the goal, it is critical that participants:

- produce sentences of four to five words without support;
- decode at a first grade level; however, instructors should feel free to modify reading requirements as necessary;
- are able to attend to a speaker (peer or adult) for at least 15 seconds; and
- are able to receptively and expressively answer simple *WH* questions (e.g., "morning" or "night" when asked a *when* question).

Ideally, *Conversation Club* instructors work with pairs of club members. We recognize, however, that it may be necessary for instructors to work with larger groups of club members, and recommend that groups not exceed four. Whenever possible, it is also helpful to match club members based on shared interests/preferred topics, since this helps make conversation more fun, meaningful, and successful.

Determining Baseline of Conversational Skill Levels

Prior to instruction, it is imperative to assess the conversational skill level of each club member at baseline to identify conversational strength areas and pinpoint compensatory strategies that may be present. The *Conversation Club* curriculum aims to target seven key goal areas which need to be mastered for an individual to engage in both successful and meaningful conversations.

- Perspective taking and social motivation
- Environmental awareness and body readiness
- Conversation initiation and topic selection
- Topic maintenance
- Active listening behaviors and attention to conversation
- Attention-gaining behaviors
- Conversation breakdown and repair strategies

Using the *Conversation Club's* Progress Report, instructors will be guided through the process of obtaining baseline data within each of these seven areas. Please see "Assessing Progress" for specific instructions regarding how to use this checklist. When gathering baseline data, we recommend that instructors set up a specific time to observe each club member engaging in child-directed conversation. It is recommended that the initial observation, as well as others throughout the program, be videotaped to help measure progress and ensure accurate data collection. Once baseline is established, this information should be used to guide intervention, determine treatment goals, and identify where to begin when implementing this curriculum. For example, if an instructor is working with a club member who has strong conversation initiation and topic selection skills, he may decide to quickly review Unit 2, in which club members are introduced to a topic, but primarily focus attention on the process of staying on topic.

Assessing Progress

The *Conversation Club's* Progress Report is a checklist for instructors to use to gather baseline data as well as monitor progress during the course of the intervention. It is recommended that instructors use the Progress Report at the start of intervention to help determine conversation goals. From there, frequency of use is at the instructor's discretion. Many instructors prefer to administer the Progress Report after each unit. Others use it to track progress at the midway point and at the end of the intervention.

Specific skills within each of the seven key domains are identified for measurement. For example, within the perspective taking and social motivation domain, club members will be asked to state one reason *why* conversations are important. Each of the skills presented on the checklist is directly correlated with the *Conversation Club's* unit progression. Instructors can find the unit within which each skill is taught listed on the Progress Report form.

Instructors should use the scale in the column on the far right of the Progress Report to aid in effectively tracking progress. The rating scale uses the following terms to define club members' mastery level within each skill area or domain: absent, emerging, developing, or mastered. Mark skills as absent when club members present understanding or use of the skill in 0% of opportunities. Mark skills as emerging when club members begin to understand or demonstrate use of the skill in less than 50% of opportunities. Mark skills as developing when club members demonstrate understanding or accurate use of the skill in 50-80% of opportunities. Finally, skills should be marked as mastered once 80% accuracy is obtained across three conversation opportunities.

It is recommended that instructors refer to the ratings when determining whether to progress to a new unit or continue instruction within the unit they are currently teaching. If instructors determine that club members have only attained an emerging understanding of the skill being taught, it is recommended that they repeat specific activities in that unit with the goal of moving club members towards mastery. Instructors should use their professional judgment to determine the readiness of club members to progress to the next unit based on club members' individual differences, strengths, and needs.

Ratings Key

M = Mastered – Performs skill independently over 80% of the time. Initiates skill with at least three different adults or peers without help, prompts, or rewards in different, appropriate settings.

D = Developing – Performs the skill independently less than 80% of the time but more than 50% of the time. Performs the skill with a limited number of peers and adults in a small number of settings. Still benefits from external reward.

E = Emerging – Initiates the skill some of the time to attain a goal or external reward. Performs the skill less than 50% of the time. Only demonstrates skill with one person in a restricted setting (i.e., therapy session).

A = Absent – Does not perform the skill.

Conversation Club Progress Report

Club Member Name:	Age:
Instructor Name:	Date:

Key: A=Absent, E=Emerging, D=Developing, M=Mastered

Targeted Conversation Skills		Rating Scale			
Perspective Taking and Social Motivation	Unit	A	E	D	M
Demonstrates motivation to have conversations with others by attempting to do at least one of the following: share information, initiate conversation, ask questions, answer questions, or use nonverbal communication (e.g., gestures).	—				
States one reason *why* conversations are important.	1				
States one reason *why* choosing topics of mutual interest is important.					
Identifies *how* conversations make others feel.	1				
Adjusts conversation based on partner's verbal or nonverbal cues (e.g., body language, tone of voice, facial expressions).	1				
Defining Conversation	Unit	A	E	D	M
States the two goals of a conversation: to *share* and *learn* about your conversation partner.	1				
States the meaning of *sharing* and *learning* during conversation.	1				
Environmental Awareness and Body Readiness	Unit	A	E	D	M
Scans the room to identify *who* is available for conversation based on nonverbal communication cues (e.g., finds an available peer).	1				
Positions body across from conversation partner at the table.	1				
Positions body at a comfortable distance for both conversation partners.	1				
Speaks with an adequate volume for conversation.	1				
Conversation Initiation and Topic Selection	Unit	A	E	D	M
Identifies the meaning of a topic as "what we like to talk about."	2				
Generates five topics.	2				
Identifies five vocabulary words associated with each preferred topic.	2				
Answers one simple WH question based on a specified topic.	2				
Initiates a conversation by asking one *what, who, where, when, why* or *how* question. What____ Who____ Where____ When____ Why____ How____	3				
Initiates a conversation by asking a question using one of the question starters: *can, would, are, did,* or *do*. Can____ Would____ Are____ Did____ Do____	7				

6 | Conversation Club

Topic Maintenance	Unit	A	E	D	M
Responds to one *who, what, where, when, why* and *how* question using related vocabulary (e.g., names a person when asked who).	3				
Creates one descriptive statement including *what, where, when,* and *who*. Includes *how* and *why* if applicable.	3				
Recalls all the information from one descriptive statement, including *what, where, when,* and *who*. Includes *how* and *why* if applicable.	3				
Without visual support, recalls all the information from one descriptive statement, including *what, where, when,* and *who*. Includes *how* and *why* if applicable.	3				
Identifies one key word (the main idea) in a statement.	4				
Uses the previously identified key word (main idea) in at least one follow-up statement.	4				
Identifies information that is missing in a statement and asks one on-topic follow-up question.	4				
Proposes more than one on-topic follow-up question and/or comment to keep the conversation going.	4				
Active Listening Behaviors and Attending to Conversation Partners	Unit	A	E	D	M
Uses nonverbal movements (e.g., head nod) to communicate that he/she is paying attention to conversation partner.	4				
"Checks in" with conversation partner's eyes.	4				
Recalls at least one detail shared by conversation partner.	6				
Recalls *who, what, where,* or *when* following a conversation.	6				
Chooses topics that are of mutual interest to both partners.	6				
Attention-Gaining Behaviors	Unit	A	E	D	M
Uses verbal and/or nonverbal communication to gain conversation partner's attention (e.g., saying name, tapping on the shoulder).	6				
Uses eye contact when gaining conversation partner's attention.	6				
Conversation Breakdown and Repair	Unit	A	E	D	M
Identifies when conversation partner is not paying attention and regains partner's attention.	5				
Uses one strategy to repair a conversation if there is a break down (e.g., repeats a statement, asks partner to repeat what he/she said).	5				
Continuing Conversations	Unit	A	E	D	M
Produces acknowledging phrases to demonstrate that he/she is paying attention (e.g., "Wow," "Neat").	7				
Changes topic in a natural manner (e.g., does not make abrupt topic changes, uses bridging statements such as, "That makes me think of…").	7				
Recalls information from a previous conversation and uses it in follow-up conversations.	7				

Scope and Sequence

The *Conversation Club* comprises eight units, each starring a character who represents a critical skill. Stories are accompanied by explicit instruction in each of the skills necessary for successful conversation.

Unit	Learning Objectives	Character
1	**Welcome to the *Conversation Club***	
	• State the goals of a conversation (e.g., to share and learn about a conversation partner) • State the meaning of sharing and learning during a conversation • State one reason why conversations are important • Scan the room to identify who is available for conversation based on nonverbal communication cues • Position body across the table from a conversation partner • Position body at a comfortable distance from a conversation partner	Friendly Freddy
2	**Selecting and Staying on Topic**	
	• Identify the meaning of a topic as "what we talk about during conversation" • Identify at least five topics without visual support • Identify at least five vocabulary words associated with each topic • Answer at least one WH question based on a given topic • State at least one reason why choosing topics of mutual interest is important	Friendly Freddy
3	**Keeping the Conversation Going**	
	• Ask and answer WH questions (*who, what, where, when, why*) • Create a descriptive statement that includes *who, what, where,* and *when* • Use a graphic organizer to recall descriptive statements including *who, what, where,* and *when* information	Paco the Parrot
4	**Using Our Eyes and Ears to Think about Our Conversation Partner**	
	• Identify a key word in partner's question/comment • Use the key word in a follow-up question/comment • Use eyes to "check in" with conversation partner • Identify whether or not conversation partner is paying attention • Use attention-gaining behaviors to gain conversation partner's	Listening Lisa and Looking Louie
5	**Conversation Repair**	
	• Identify if there is a conversation breakdown • Determine the cause of the conversation breakdown • Select a strategy to repair the conversation breakdown	Fix It Farrah
6	**Remembering What Our Conversation Partner Says**	
	• Use strategies to improve memory and recall • Create a mental picture of a statement made during a conversation • Choose a topic of mutual interest • Recall *who, what, where,* or *when* following a conversation • Identify whether or not conversation partner is paying attention • Use attention-gaining behaviors to gain conversation partner's attention (e.g., saying partner's name, tapping partner on the shoulder)	Good Memory Maria

7	**Expanding the Depth and Breadth of Conversation**	
	• Use a variety of new question words (e.g., *do, can, will*) to initiate and sustain conversation • Use previously learned active listening strategies to determine if information was interesting or not • Produce an acknowledging phrase (e.g., *Wow!*) after hearing a comment or story a club member finds interesting • Change a topic • Use a bridging statement when shifting topics • Recall more than one topic that was introduced during the conversation	New Words Nate
8	**Bringing It All Together**	
	• Propose more than one on-topic follow-up question and/or comment to keep the conversation going • Acknowledge and integrate a shift in the topic or subtopics of conversation • Recall information from a previous conversation and use it in follow-up conversations • Identify a subtopic and make a bridging statement or question to shift the conversation	All Club Members

Context for Delivering Instruction

The *Conversation Club* curriculum was originally intended to be delivered during lunch time. Over time, instruction has been expanded to include other available times, depending on club members' schedules. For example, *Conversation Club* instruction may take place as part of an after-school program or as a component of a social skills class.

Structure and Pacing of Units and Activities

The *Conversation Club* curriculum is made up of eight units, each including the following information:

	What Will Club Members Learn? – Describes the key skills addressed in each unit.	
	Why Do We Teach This? – Describes the underlying rationale for teaching each skill, and how the skill fits into the overarching goal of becoming a better conversationalist	
	Outcome Objectives – Lists the goals of each unit (i.e., what club members should "know" by the end of the unit)	
	Reinforcement – Identifies which behaviors should be reinforced during the unit	
	Activity List – Provides a list of the activities included in the unit	

At the beginning of each unit, the instructor uses one of the *Conversation Club* characters as an anchor for introducing the specific conversation skill being targeted. In order to increase intrinsic motivation, instructors also provide a meaningful rationale for learning the skill. During the unit, instructors describe and model the activities; each activity is designed to facilitate mastery of a targeted skill. The progression of activities provides scaffolded opportunities for practice.

Each unit contains a selection of activities, including stories and games, which support the teaching of the target conversation skill. Each activity is described in detail, including the following:

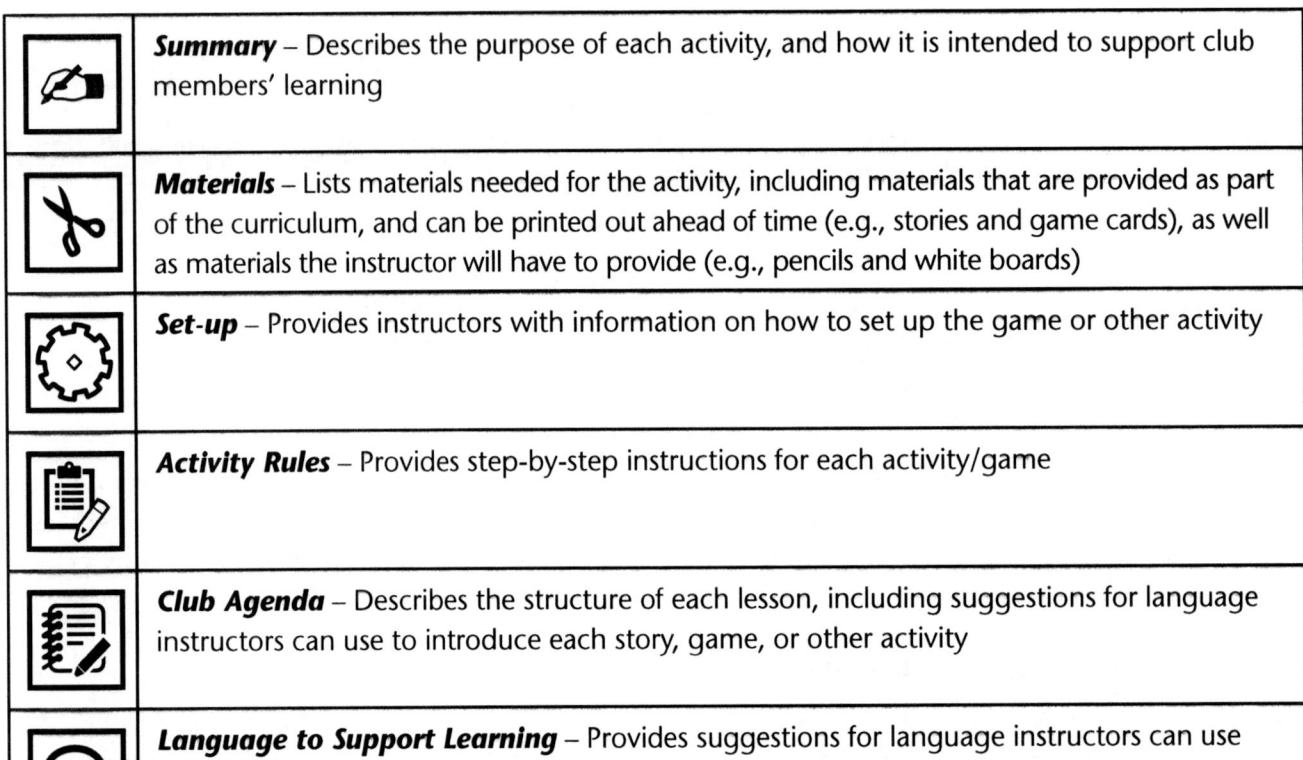

	Summary – Describes the purpose of each activity, and how it is intended to support club members' learning
	Materials – Lists materials needed for the activity, including materials that are provided as part of the curriculum, and can be printed out ahead of time (e.g., stories and game cards), as well as materials the instructor will have to provide (e.g., pencils and white boards)
	Set-up – Provides instructors with information on how to set up the game or other activity
	Activity Rules – Provides step-by-step instructions for each activity/game
	Club Agenda – Describes the structure of each lesson, including suggestions for language instructors can use to introduce each story, game, or other activity
	Language to Support Learning – Provides suggestions for language instructors can use when praising club members for using their conversation skills

Conversation skills are gradually introduced over the course of the program, and club members should be given frequent opportunities (15–20 minute periods three to four times each week) to practice new skills. Since these skills are intended to build on one another over time, it is important for instructors to spiral back to reinforce earlier skills. This helps to ensure that they will be integrated rather than forgotten.

Although *Conversation Club* is designed as a sequential program to be taught multiple times a week over the course of an academic year, instructors should feel free to adapt the program based on their club members' unique strengths and needs, as well as staffing availability. For example, if club members are having a difficult time mastering specific skills (e.g., understanding how to use *WH* words), instructors should feel free to repeat the same lesson until club members are ready to move on. On the other hand, for club members who are more capable conversationalists, instructors may wish to combine and/or skip lessons that seem unnecessary. The Progress Report should be used to determine club members' strengths and needs. Regardless of which lessons instructors decide to teach, it is highly recommended that Unit 1 not be skipped. It introduces club members to the concept of what a club is, and to the Conversation Club specifically. Each lesson plan provides suggested language for teaching. However, instructors should adapt or modify the instructional language based on the individual needs of each club member.

Making Lessons Fun

In order to secure buy-in from club members and make lessons more fun, seven *Conversation Club* characters were created to teach the conversation skills targeted in the curriculum:

- *Friendly Freddy* – President of the Conversation Club; his character teaches club members the meaning of a conversation and why conversations are important
- *Paco the Parrot* – Friendly Freddy's best friend; he wants club members to use his favorite words (*who, what, where, when,* and *why*) to keep the conversation going
- *Listening Lisa* – helps club members identify key words from their partner's speech and use these words to keep the conversation going
- *Looking Louie* – helps club members use their eyes to "check in" with their conversation partners and make sure they are paying attention
- *Fix It Farrah* – helps club members identify and repair conversation breakdowns
- *Good Memory Maria* – helps club members visualize what their partners are saying and remember what was said
- *New Words Nate* – helps club members expand their conversation using phrases like, "Could you…"; "Would you…"; "Did you…"; and, "Are you…"; and continue conversation by using bridging statements such as, "That makes me think of…" and acknowledging phrases like, "Cool!" and "Wow!"

Conversation Club members have a clubhouse, secret passwords, and club rules that help guide interactions. Throughout the program, these characters serve as reminders of specific conversation skills and how to use them. They give club members something to hook concepts onto, and allow instructors to prompt club members with questions such as, *"What would Friendly Freddy want us to say?"* The *Conversation Club* characters are intended to be highly motivating for club members, making activities seem more like games than lessons and making the program more culturally relatable. *Conversation Club* characters can also be referenced outside of club time to promote generalization of conversation skills across the school day.

Reinforcing Effort and Engagement

The *Conversation Club* curriculum combines both extrinsic and intrinsic motivators. In terms of extrinsic motivation, a reinforcement sheet is included in each unit. The reinforcement sheet reflects the skills addressed in that unit as well as the skills taught in previous units. During instructional sessions, instructors to keep track of each time club members display one of the listed skills by awarding them a tally mark on the reinforcement sheet. This immediate visual feedback helps club members identify important skills and motivates them to continue demonstrating target skills. It is up to the instructor to determine the best way to make use of the points earned. Instructors have found several different systems that have worked for them. For example, if you already have a classroom system, it might make sense to merge the systems. Another option is set a goal for the club members for each session. For example, "If you each earn 10 tally marks, you can earn lunch with a favorite friend or teacher." Other groups have found it motivating to set a group goal that accumulates across sessions. For example, "When we reach 100 points, we will earn a Conversation Club party." The key to any system is that the reinforcement must be immediate, specific, and meaningful. We encourage the selection of reinforcers that promote opportunities for meaningful interactions with peers.

Although extrinsic motivation is an important way of "hooking" club members' attention, this is not the only way the *Conversation Club* nurtures club member engagement. Teaching the "why" of conversation is at the heart of the *Conversation Club*. Opportunities to discuss why conversation is important (e.g., conversations are fun, we get to share information, we get to ask questions and learn things about our friends, good conversations make people want to spend time with us) are woven throughout each lesson. One of the key concepts infused throughout the curriculum is that thinking about our partners, selecting topics based on their interests, and asking questions that show we are paying attention when they talk gives people "good/nice thoughts." Likewise, it gives us good/nice thoughts when people pay attention to what we are saying.

Tips and Troubleshooting (or Making Modifications)

The following tips help instructors troubleshoot problems and/or make any necessary modifications:

- **My club members can demonstrate the skills during the lessons but do not generalize them to other times of the day.**

    Identify opportunities to connect *Conversation Club* language and skills to other times during the day (e.g., during lunch, while children are conversing, use *WH* words to support comprehension in language arts). A list of generalization opportunities" is supplied at the end of each unit.

    Extend a lesson over more than one session. The *Conversation Club* is flexible, and pacing should be determined based on the needs of club members. Instructors should feel free to repeat, skip, or modify a lesson based on the learning level of club members.

- **My students are not motivated to be part of the Conversation Club.**

    Do not forget: these students have been selected to be part of the club because they need support in learning the skills necessary to carry on a conversation. When something is hard, it is not likely to be seen as fun. This is where the reinforcement system becomes critically important. Initially, conversing may not be intrinsically rewarding for club members, so we need to identify something that is motivating. Instructors should make sure the external reinforcement opportunities are highly motivating for club members.

    Have fun! These lessons are designed to be fun and engaging. If there is a topic or a theme that is engaging to club members, capitalize on it. There is no reason to stick to our prescribed topics and activities. For example, in Unit 3: Lesson 3, club members ask *WH* questions to uncover the secret picture their partner is holding. If club members are interested in *Star Wars*, swap out our pictures for the Death Star and C-3PO.

- **How do I know when it is time to move on and teach the next conversation skill?**

    The curriculum includes a progress monitoring sheet. This supports instructors in determining the strengths and needs of club members and provides objective data to aid in selecting the skills to target for instruction. At the beginning of each unit, instructors should familiarize themselves with the outcome objectives. This will provide them with a clear sense of the specific skills they are addressing.

Instructors will also want to pay close attention to club member behaviors as they move through a lesson. What type of prompting is needed? Do club members require verbal or visual reminders to demonstrate the skills, or are they displaying them independently? Finally, we recommend that instructors identify specific opportunities during the day when they would expect to see club members display key conversation behaviors. Are they able to do so independently? Thinking through all of these questions will help instructors determine when it is time to move on.

*Make sure to read the suggestions at the end of each unit, under the heading: "If club members are having a difficult time with one or more goals, you might want to consider…"

Unit 1: Welcome to the Conversation Club

 What Will Club Members Learn?

Club members will learn about the Conversation Club and its purpose, and will meet the club president, Friendly Freddy. They will find out what a club is, select a password, review club rules, and be introduced to the reinforcement system. Activities will focus on teaching what a conversation is and why it is important, how conversation makes us feel, and how to get ready for conversation by identifying available conversation partners, orienting our bodies in the direction of our conversation partners, and using our indoor voices.

 Why Do We Teach This?

The core goal of this unit is to help club members identify and explore the underlying purpose of a conversation: to share and learn information. Successful conversations rely on the readiness of conversation partners to acknowledge one another, read each other's social cues, and think about each other's needs and interests. Children with social learning deficits often do not use nonverbal communication skills to reference their conversation partners, check to see if their conversation partners are listening, or assess their partners' interest in the conversation. As a result, conversation may seem one-sided; and the child with social learning deficits may speak at length about his personal interests and fail to monitor his partner's reactions. By studying the elements of a conversation and why they are important, club members will gain a deeper understanding of the benefits of using conversation to share and learn about others. Furthermore, children with social cognition deficits also require explicit instruction in how to prepare for conversation, such as how to position their bodies appropriately for and during discourse and identify possible conversation partners — skills which are necessary for laying the groundwork for successful conversations.

 Outcome Objectives

This unit teaches club members to do the following:

- State the purpose of a conversation (i.e., to share and learn about your conversation partner)
- State the meaning of sharing and learning during a conversation
- State one reason why conversations are important
- Scan the room to identify who is available for conversation based on nonverbal communication cues

- Position their bodies across from their conversation partner at the table
- Position their bodies at a comfortable distance from their conversation partner

 Reinforcement

Provide one point each time club members:

- Share space by sitting or standing at an appropriate distance
- Ask on-topic questions
- Answer on-topic questions

 Activity List

1. *Storybooks:* "Welcome to the Conversation Club!"
2. Getting Ready for Conversation Game
3. "Who or What Is in My Space?"
4. "Who Am I?" Game

Activities

 ### Activity 1: "Welcome to the Conversation Club!" Story

 Summary

Each unit begins with a story. The purpose of the story is to introduce club members to the new concepts covered during the unit. Feel free to reread this story as you move through the lessons in Unit 1. In "Welcome to the Conversation Club," club members are introduced to the Conversation Club and meet their illustrious club president, Friendly Freddy. Club members have the opportunity to create their own password and learn the rules that will help the club be successful. With Freddy's help, club members will define what a conversation is, learn about the different ways we communicate with one another, and think about how conversation makes us feel.

Instructors will model examples of methods for club members to gain each other's attention.

 Materials

- *Storybooks:* "Welcome to the Conversation Club!"
- Unit 1 Reinforcement Page

Talking Points for Instructor:

"You are about to learn about a special new club that we want you to be a part of. To learn all about it, listen carefully to the story I am about to read."

Club Agenda

1. Introduce activity.
2. Read "Welcome to the Conversation Club!"
3. Add club members' points.
4. Wrap up.

 Language to Support Learning

"Great job being a part of the group and sitting at the table!"

"You are doing a great job participating in the club by answering questions. Friendly Freddy would be so proud."

Unit 1: Welcome to the *Conversation Club* | 15

Activity 2: Getting Ready for Conversation Game Summary

Summary

This activity is designed to help club members practice positioning themselves to have a conversation. Use the Friendly Freddy icon to illustrate and review with club members what they need to do to get ready for a conversation. First, Freddy always checks to see who is in his space. Second, he decides if it is someone he wants to talk to and adjusts his body position to make sure he is looking at that person, and that she can see him. Finally, once he is looking at the person, and she is looking at him, he makes sure he is standing close enough to use his indoor voice.

 ## Materials

- Getting Ready for Conversation Game Cards – Movement Cards, pages 1–2; Question Cards, pages 1–3; and Visual Reminder Card (all cut out ahead of time)
- Getting Ready for Conversation Game Materials – Game Rules
- Getting Ready for Conversation Game Visual Reminder
- Unit 1 Reinforcement Page

 ## Set-up

Instructor places two card piles on the table: one pile of Movement Cards and one pile of Question Cards.

 ## Activity Rules

1. Player 1 picks up one Movement Card. Player 1 reads the card and completes the movement described on the card (e.g., "Skip to the corner"). Player 1 stays in the corner and waits for Player 2.

2. Player 2 picks up one Question Card. Player 2 reads the card, then uses the Activity Rules visual to then finds Player 1 and uses the visual reminder to help ask the question. The instructor reinforces players for demonstrating targeted behaviors (e.g., maintaining expected proximity, using an indoor voice, waiting for peers to look at them).

3. Player 2 goes first the next time, selecting one Movement Card, and so on.

4. Club members earn points for positioning their body to be near their partner, "checking in" with their eyes (e.g., looking at their partner when speaking and listening), and using their indoor voice.

16 | Conversation Club

Talking Points for Instructor:

"Club members, Friendly Freddy has a challenge for us; he wants us to play a game. The object of the game is to find your partner wherever he ends up in the room and ask your question. You will earn a point for each time you move your body to be near your partner, use your eyes to think about your partner, or use an indoor voice to ask your question."

Club Agenda

1. Have club members recite the password.
2. Review: Who is Friendly Freddy? What does Friendly Freddy want us to do? What is a club? What is conversation?
3. Reread "Welcome to the Conversation Club!" (optional).
4. Introduce game.
5. Play game.
6. Add club members' points.
7. Wrap Up.

 Language to Support Learning

"I could tell you were thinking about Marianna because you "checked in" with your eyes and moved your body towards her."

"Great job moving your body close to Mae and using your eyes to look at her."

Unit 1: Welcome to the *Conversation Club* | 17

Activity 3: "Who or What Is in My Space?" Game

 ## Summary

This activity is designed to help club members scan their environment for increased awareness of *who* and *what* is around them. Freddy always looks around the room. He always wants to know *who* is part of the group, if his body looks "ready for conversation," and *what* else is nearby. If Freddy sees that another club member is wearing a shirt with a picture of an animal on it, he now knows that his peer may like animals or want to talk about animals. During this activity, club members will use their eyes to check for *who* and *what* is in their space.

 ## Materials

- "Who or What Is in My Space?" Game Cards, pages 1–3 (cut out in advance)
- Piece of paper with two columns, labeled WHO and WHAT
- Unit 1 Reinforcement Page

 ## Set-up

Instructor places the WHO and WHAT cards from the "Who or What Is in My Space?" Game Cards in a pile on a table and prepares a piece of paper or white board with the words WHO and WHAT written at the top.

 ## Activity Rules

1. Club members take turns picking up a card. Player 1 scans and describes while Player 2 listens, scans, and finds.

2. Instructor demonstrates what is expected when a player chooses a card.

3. WHO card – When this card is drawn, the player (Player 1) scans the room and chooses one person in her space. She then uses the clues page to describe the person (e.g., what the person is wearing, whether the person is a boy or girl, something the person likes) to Player 2. Player 2 guesses *who* Player 1 is describing.

4. WHAT card – When this card is drawn, the player (Player 1) reads the key detail (e.g., "Find something that is red"). The player scans the room to find an object (e.g., "red shirt") in her space. After choosing an object based on the required detail, she uses the clues page to describe the object to Player 2. Player 2 guesses *what* Player 1 is talking about, then writes the name of the object on the "WHO/WHAT" page underneath the WHAT column.

5. After the *who* or *what* has been guessed and written down, it is the next player's turn to draw a card, etc.

6. Club members earn a point each time they scan the room and answer a question. Points are kept on the teachers' tally sheet.

18 | Conversation Club

Talking Points for Instructor:

"Club members, Friendly Freddy has another game for us to play. The object of the game is to check out 'who' and 'what' is around you at the table or in the room. This means checking out your space. You will earn a point on our point sheet each time you (a) pick up a card, (b) scan the room, and (c) find 'who' or 'what' is in your space."

Club Agenda

1. Have club members recite the password.
2. Review: Who is Friendly Freddy? What does Friendly Freddy want us to do? What is a club? What is conversation? What is an indoor voice?
3. Reread "Welcome to the Conversation Club!" (optional).
4. Play game.
5. Add club members' points.
6. Wrap up.

 Language to Support Learning

"I could tell you were checking your space because you used your eyes to look around the room."

"I could tell you were thinking about Miguel, because you "checked in" with your eyes and listened to his words."

Unit 1: Welcome to the *Conversation Club* | 19

Activity 4: "Who Am I?" Game

 Summary

This game is designed to reinforce that a conversation is when two or more people share and learn information. Students use verbal and nonverbal communication to give information about an animal that their partners cannot see (*sharing* information). Their partners have to use their eyes and ears to guess the correct animal (*learning* information).

 Materials

- "Who Am I?" Game Picture Cards (cut out in advance)
- "Who Am I" Game Action Die Cutout (cut and folded in advance)
- Unit 1 Reinforcement Page

 Set-up

Instructor places a pile of picture cards and the action die on the table. If the players need help, the instructor can provide a list of animal options.

 Activity Rules

1. Player 1 picks up a Picture Card. Player 1 should not show the card to Player 2.
2. Player 1 rolls the Action Die and follows the direction on the die (e.g., act it out, make a noise, give a clue).
3. Player 2 attempts to guess the animal based on the sound, action, or clue.
4. Player 1 continues to roll the die and follow the instructions until Player 2 is able to guess the animal.
5. Player 2 goes next, rolling the die and following the directions on the die, and so on.
6. Players earn points two ways: for giving information about their animal and for making guesses based on their partners' clues.

    * Monitor closely to ensure that the players are using their words and their actions to share and learn information.

Talking Points for Instructor:

"Freddy has a brand new challenge for us. He wants you to share information with your partner by giving him clues. You will use your words and your movements to help him guess or learn which animal you are thinking about. You will earn a point for giving clues, and your partner will earn a point for making a guess about the animal you are describing."

Club Agenda

1. Have club members recite the password.
2. Review: What does Friendly Freddy want us to do? What is a club? What is conversation? Why does Freddy want us to "check in" with our eyes? Where should our body be during conversation?
3. Reread "Welcome to the Conversation Club!" (optional).
4. Play game.
5. Add club members' points.
6. Wrap up.

 Language to Support Learning

"I could tell you were thinking about me, because you looked at me and moved your body near me."

"Your words helped me think about the animal you were describing."

Unit 1: Welcome to the *Conversation Club* | 21

Generalization Opportunities

During the day, highlight when club members are hanging out and talking together, and how they are enjoying the experience with one another (e.g., *"I can tell you and Bobby are really enjoying talking together about soccer"*).

Praise club members when they orient their bodies toward their peers during conversation, and for asking and answering on-topic questions (e.g., *"Sarah knows you are thinking about her because you are looking at her and your body is facing hers"*).

Notice and highlight when club members are sharing and learning information during conversation with one another (e.g., *"Your words just helped Jake learn all about the game you are playing"*).

If club members are having a difficult time with one or more goals, you might want to consider:

- Repeating an activity
- Modifying an existing activity
- Looking ahead to future activities to see if that skill is practiced in other lessons
- Creating additional practice opportunities during group activity and/or throughout the school day

Materials

**Unit 1
Activity 2:
Getting Ready for
Conversation Game**

 Activity Rules

Player 1:

- Pick up one Movement Card.
- Read the card.
- Do the movement (e.g., skip to the corner).

Player 2:

- Pick up one Question Card.
- Read the card.
- Find Player 1 and ask the question.
- Remember to use an indoor voice, check your space, and look at the other player.

To continue play:

- Alternate turns, with Player 2 drawing a Movement Card next and Player 1 drawing the Question Card, and so on.
- Have fun!

Unit 1, Activity 2 Materials:
Getting Ready for Conversation Game Movement Cards

Skip to the corner of the room	Hop to the door
Leap to the front of the room	Roll to the middle of the rooms
Dance to the clock	Shake and twist your body to the closet
Sit under a chair in the room	Twirl across the room until you are standing behind an adult

Unit 1, Activity 2 Materials:
Getting Ready for Conversation Game Question Cards

What do you like to watch on TV?	Do you play video games?
Do you play sports?	What is your favorite color?
Do you have pets?	How old are you?
Do you have any brothers or sisters?	What is your favorite food?
Where do you live?	What is your teacher's name?
What color is your shirt?	Do you like to draw or color?

Unit 1, Activity 2 Materials:
Getting Ready for Conversation Game Visual Reminder

Don't forget:

Use indoor voice

Check your space

Look with your eyes

Don't forget:

Use indoor voice

Check your space

Look with your eyes

Don't forget:

Use indoor voice

Check your space

Look with your eyes

Don't forget:

Use indoor voice

Check your space

Look with your eyes

26 | Conversation Club

**Unit 1, Activity 3 Materials:
"Who or What Is in My Space?" Game Cards Page 1 of 3**

WHO
Find a person who is in your space

WHO
Find a person who is in your space

WHO
Find a person who is in your space

WHO
Find a person who is in your space

Unit 1, Activity 3 Materials:
"Who or What Is in My Space?" Game Cards Page 2 of 3

WHAT Find something that is the COLOR RED 	**WHAT** Find something that is the COLOR BLUE 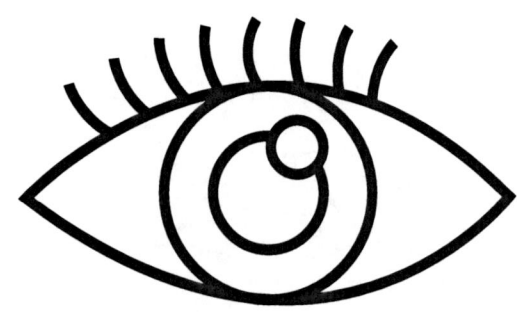
WHAT Find something that is the COLOR GREEN 	**WHAT** Find something that is the COLOR ORANGE  

Unit 1, Activity 3 Materials:
"Who or What Is in My Space?" Game Cards Page 3 of 3

WHAT Find something that is **BIG**	**WHAT** Find something that is **SMALL**
WHAT Find a **FOOD**	**WHAT** Find a **DRINK**

Unit 1: Welcome to the *Conversation Club* | 29

**Unit 1, Activity 4 Materials:
"Who Am I?" Game Picture Cards Page 1 of 3**

Cat
Act: Pretend to lick your hand
Noise: MEOW
Clue: Loves to purr

Dog
Act: Pretend to wag your tail
Noise: WOOF! WOOF!
Clue: Likes to play fetch

Mouse
Act: Pretend to eat cheese
Noise: SQUEAK
Clue: Loves to eat cheese

Horse
Act: Stand on hands and legs; pretend to eat grass
Noise: NEIGH
Clue: Can give rides to kids and adults

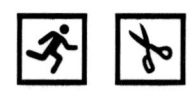

Unit 1, Activity 4 Materials:
"Who Am I?" Game Picture Cards Page 2 of 3

Monkey
Act: Pretend to swing arms side to side while low to the ground
Noise: OOHOOHAAHAHH
Clue: Swings from trees

Lion
Act: Pretend to roar without making a noise
Noise: ROARRRR
Clue: A very big cat that likes to roar

Duck
Act: Pretend to waddle
Noise: QUACK
Clue: Swims in ponds

Bear
Act: Stand up, arms above your head, and make a mean face
Noise: GRRRRROWL
Clue: A very scary animal that eats fish

**Unit 1, Activity 4 Materials:
"Who Am I?" Game Picture Cards Page 3 of 3**

Sheep
Act: Stand on hands and feet, hop around
Noise: BAAAA
Clue: Lives on a farm and has white fur

Bird
Act: Use arms for wings and pretend to fly
Noise: CHIRP CHIRP
Clue: Eats worms and flies in the sky

Seal
Act: Lie on belly, pick up head, and clap hands
Noise: ARR! ARR! ARR! ARR!
Clue: Lives in the cold and loves to swim

Owl
Act: Use arms for wings and fly
Noise: WHOO WHOO
Clue: A bird that flies at night

**Unit 1, Activity 4 Materials:
"Who Am I?" Game Action Cutout**

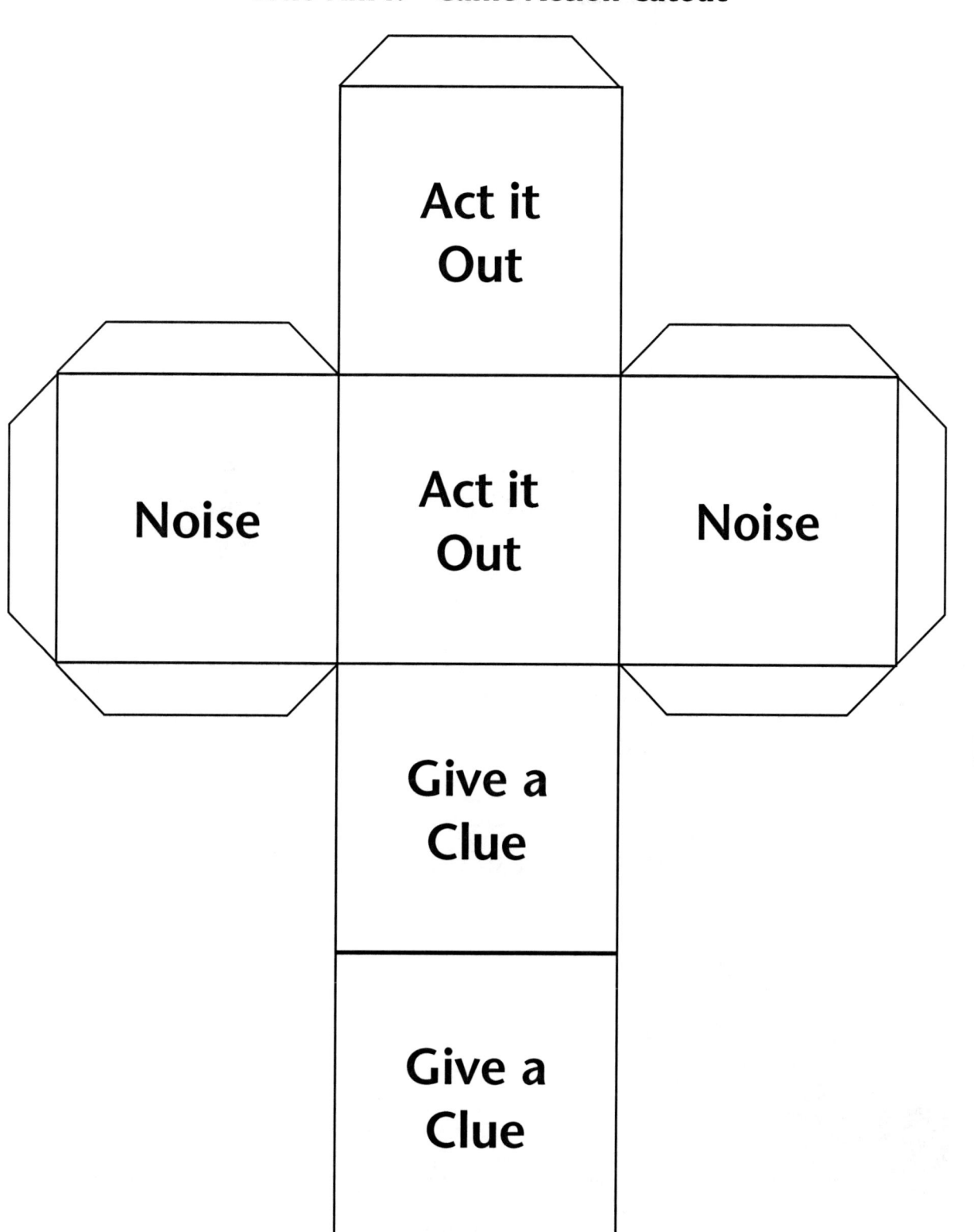

	Act it Out	
Noise	Act it Out	Noise
	Give a Clue	
	Give a Clue	

Unit 1: Welcome to the *Conversation Club* | 33

Unit 1: Reinforcement Page

Name:	Name:	Name:
Share Space	Share Space	Share Space
Answer Questions ?	Answer Questions ?	Answer Questions ?
Ask Questions	Ask Questions	Ask Questions

Unit 2: Selecting and Staying on Topic

What Will Club Members Learn?

Club members will learn what a topic is (i.e., "what we talk about during conversation"). They will also learn that Friendly Freddy wants us to have conversations and stay on topic. By the end of the unit, we expect club members to understand why it is important to select topics their conversation partner likes to talk about and how it makes their conversation partners feel when they select topics of interest to them.

Why Do We Teach This?

The core goals of this unit are to help club members understand the meaning and purpose of choosing and discussing a topic during conversation. Children with social cognitive deficits often initiate conversation based on a few highly preferred topics and use repetitive vocabulary or phrases when navigating the interaction. Club members will learn an organized way to think about semantic associations and categorization in the context of a conversation. Teaching club members what a topic is, expanding on the number of topics and vocabulary in their lexicon, and providing learning opportunities to remain on topic will have a positive impact on club members' abilities to formulate organized, coherent thoughts and will result in more positive interactions with their peers.

Outcome Objectives

This unit teaches club members to do the following:
- Identify the meaning of a topic as "what we talk about during conversation"
- Identify at least five topics without visual support
- Identify at least five vocabulary words associated with each topic
- Answer at least one WH question based on a given topic
- State at least one reason why choosing topics of mutual interest is important

Reinforcement

Provide one point each time club members:
- Share space by sitting or standing at an appropriate distance
- Ask on-topic questions
- Answer on-topic questions
- Generate a topic

Activity List

1. *Storybooks:* "What Will We Talk About?"
2. "What is a Topic?" Game
3. Topic Bonanza Game
4. Topic Card Game

Activities

Activity 1: "What Will We Talk About?" Story

Summary

The purpose of the story is to introduce club members to the concept of a topic. A topic is defined as *"what we talk about during conversation."* The story also illustrates the importance of selecting topics that our conversation partners like. When we select topics that are of interest to both ourselves and others, our peers will be more likely to want to talk with us in the future. Feel free to reread this story as club members move through the lessons in Unit 2.

Materials

- *Storybooks*: "What Will We Talk About?"
- Unit 2 Reinforcement Page

Talking Points for Instructor:

"Friendly Freddy and the Conversation Club are back again, but this time there is a real problem in the clubhouse: no one is talking! It's up to us to help them figure out why and what they can do to fix it."

Club Agenda

1. Have club members recite the password.
2. Review: Who is Friendly Freddy? What does Friendly Freddy want us to do? What is a club?
3. Introduce activity.
4. Read "What Will We Talk About?"
5. Add club members' points.
6. Wrap up.

Language to Support Learning

"Those are great topic suggestions. They will definitely get the club members talking again."

"Thank you for contributing to our conversation. I learned a lot from what you shared."

Activity 2: "What is a Topic?" Game

Summary

Using Friendly Freddy and a club member as a model, the instructor will create a visual of what the conversation process looks like. The purpose of this visual is to illustrate that the words we use, as well as the topics we discuss, help our conversation partners think about the same topic.

Materials

- "What Is a Topic?" Game cards, pages 1–3 (cut out ahead of time)
- Thought bubbles – laminated, or enough copies for each club member to respond to each peer
- Dry erase marker for each club member
- Unit 2 Reinforcement Page

Set-up

Instructor places the Game Cards on the table. Each club member receives a laminated Thought Bubble and a dry erase marker.

Activity Rules

1. Hand out a Thought Bubble and dry erase marker to each player.
2. Player 1 selects a Game Card and describes what is on the card (e.g., "I am thinking about an animal with four legs and lots of fur, who says, 'woof'").
3. Player 2 writes the topic being described onto his Thought Bubble, then holds it up (e.g., "dog"). Repeat the process until everyone has had a turn.
4. Club members earn points for sharing a topic and answering a partner's question over the topic.

Talking Points for Instructor:

"The object of this activity is to use our words to describe a topic and help our conversation partners think about the same topic. (Demonstrate while drawing Freddy having a conversation — see visual.) We have conversations to talk about things we like and to learn new things. Things that we talk about are called topics. When we share what we know about a topic, the other person learns about the topic. You will be earning points for sharing your thoughts about a topic with your partner and answering questions about the topic."

Club Agenda

1. Have club members recite the password.
2. Review: What does Friendly Freddy want us to do? What is a club? Why do we have conversations with people?
3. Reread "What Will We Talk About?" (optional).
4. Introduce activity.
5. Play game.
6. Add club members' points.
7. Wrap up.

Language to Support Learning

"Your words made your friend think of the topic you were describing."

38 | Conversation Club

Activity 3: Topic Bonanza Game

Summary

This game is designed to help club members generate topics for conversations and to illustrate the wide range of topics they can and do talk about.

Materials

- White board or piece of paper
- Unit 2 Reinforcement Page

Set-up

Use a piece of paper or white board to record answers. Make sure all club members can see the white board. If you think club members will have a difficult time generating topics on their own, bring visuals (e.g., magazines, pictures, etc.) that might help them generate ideas.

Talking Points for Instructor:

"We know that as president of our club, Friendly Freddy wants us to have conversations. And we know that people have conversations about topics. To make sure we are ready to have great conversations, Friendly Freddy came up with a game to help us think about all of the topics we could possibly talk about. The object of the game is for you to name as many topics as you can. Our goal is to identify 10 topics. Remember: each time you suggest a topic, you will earn a point on our conversation tracking sheet."

Club Agenda

1. Have club members recite the password.
2. Review: What does Friendly Freddy want us to do? What do we do in the Conversation Club? How can you help your conversation partner think about the same topic as you?
3. Reread "What Will We Talk About?" (optional).
4. Introduce activity.
5. Play game.
6. Add club members' points.
7. Wrap up.

Language to Support Learning

"Thank you for sharing all of those topics. There are so many topics we can talk about together."

Unit 2: Selecting and Staying on Topic | 39

Activity 4: Topic Card Game

Summary

This game is designed to help club members practice asking and answering on-topic questions using topic cards.

Materials

- Topic Card Game cards (pages 1–5, cut out in advance)
- Unit 2 Reinforcement Page

Set-up

Place the Topic Cards in the center of the table.

Activity Rules

1. Player 1 picks up a card and reads the question to Player 2.
2. Player 2 answers the question.
3. Next, Player 2 draws a card and reads the question to Player 1; play continues as players take alternate turns.
4. Club members earn points for asking and answering questions.

Talking Points for Instructor:

"Friendly Freddy was super impressed with all of the topics you came up with. Now he wants us to practice having conversations about some of those wonderful topics. The object of this activity is to practice asking your partner questions, and answering questions from your partner with on-topic responses. You will earn points for each question you ask and each on-topic answer you give."

Club Agenda

1. Have club members recite the password.
2. Review: What is a topic? Let's name three topics people can talk about in conversation. Have you had any conversations today? What were they about?
3. Reread "What Will We Talk About?" (optional).
4. Introduce activity.
5. Play game.
6. Add club members' points.
7. Wrap up.

Language to Support Learning

"I really like the way you listened to your partner's question and gave an on-topic answer!"

"What was the topic that question was about?"

40 | Conversation Club

Activity 5: Super Brainstorm

Summary

This activity is designed to help club members increase their fund of knowledge around a given topic. As a result, club members will expand their thinking, questioning skills, and vocabulary related to that topic.

Materials

- White board or piece of paper
- Unit 2 Reinforcement Page
- Super Brainstorm Worksheet Board

Set-up

Use the Super Brainstorm Worksheet Board of your choice to record answers. Make sure all club members can see the white board. If you think students will have a difficult time generating topics on their own, bring visuals (e.g., magazines, pictures, etc.) that might help them generate ideas.

Activity Rules

1. Ask club members to identify one topic.
2. Ask club members to identify as many words or phrases related to that topic as they can.
3. Optional: Set a goal for how many related words you want club members to identify.
4. Club members earn points for sharing space during the conversation and for adding details about the given topic.

Talking Points for Instructor:

"Remember that Friendly Freddy has another trick up his sleeve to help us have good conversations. When we think about things we want to talk about, he wants us to have a super brainstorm. The super brainstorm will help us think of all of the things we know about the topic and help make our conversation more interesting. When our conversation is more interesting and we expand what we talk about, people will want to hang out with us and talk to us. You will earn points for sharing space in the conversation and adding details to our topic."

Club Agenda

1. Have club members recite the password.
2. Review: Who is in the Conversation Club? What do you like to talk about in conversations? Think back to the last activity; what did you learn about another Conversation Club member?
3. Reread "What Will We Talk About?" (optional).
4. Introduce activity.
5. Play game.
6. Add club members' points.
7. Wrap up.

Language to Support Learning

"We know so much about that topic. We are going to have a great conversation about video games."

"All this information about soccer will make our conversation so interesting."

Activity 6: Conversation Club

Summary

The goal of this lesson is to help club members recognize that to make conversations enjoyable, we need to think about topics that interest our partners. In this lesson, club members will interview each other to create Conversation Club files that reflect their partners' interests. Club members will use this information in future conversations to help them generate topic ideas when talking with these partners.

Materials

- Conversation Club Files
- Unit 2 Reinforcement Page

Set-up

Give each club member, including the instructor, a blank Conversation Club member file.

Activity Rules

1. Model asking a club member a question using her Conversation Club file.
2. Club members take turns asking each other questions using Conversation Club files. Optional: use visuals for each question to provide options for students who have difficulty with recall.
3. Club members earn points for asking questions, giving answers, and sharing space during an exchange.

Talking Points for Instructor:

"Freddy loves it when we have conversations. Conversations can be a lot of fun when we get to talk about things we are interested in. Talking about things we are interested in makes us feel good. When we talk about things that other club members are interested in, it makes them feel good, and they will want to keep talking with us. We are going to learn more about each other today, so we can have conversations that we all enjoy. You will be earning points for asking and answering on-topic questions and sharing space during our conversation."

Club Agenda

1. Have club members recite the password.
2. Review: What does Friendly Freddy want us to do? Do you like having conversations? What do you like to talk about? If you were talking about recess, what is something you could talk about?
3. Reread "What Will We Talk About?" (optional).
4. Introduce activity.
5. Do activity.
6. Add club members' points.
7. Wrap up.

Language to Support Learning

"I can tell talking about Halloween made your partner feel good."

Generalization Opportunities

During naturally occurring conversations in class, highlight when club members share information and reflect on a topic they bring up: *"I really enjoyed that conversation about football, and I learned a lot from the information you shared."*

During question and answer opportunities, highlight and praise when club members stay on topic: *"Great job staying on topic. Freddy would be so proud!"*

Write a phrase or a word on the board or piece of paper and ask club members to think of as many words as they can related to that topic (e.g., summer: beach, pool, no school).

Highlight when you or other club members are making a decision to talk about or do something based on another person's interests: *"Billy chose to play Legos because he knows James loves Legos, and he really likes playing with James."*

If club members are having a difficult time with one or more goals, you might want to consider:

- Repeating an activity
- Modifying an existing activity
- Providing visuals if students are having trouble generating topics
- Choosing a book or video about a topic (e.g., football — discuss all of the details and information related to the topic) for students who are having trouble generating information about a topic

Materials

Unit 2, Activity 2 Materials:
"What is a Topic?" Game Page 1 of 3

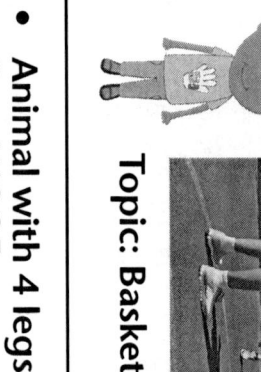

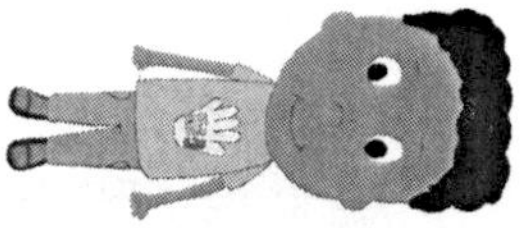

Topic: Basketball
- Played on a court
- Uses an orange ball
- Shoot into a hoop
- Play on a team

Topic: Dog
- Animal with 4 legs
- Says WOOF
- Some have tails

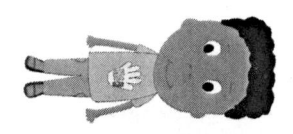

Topic: Lion
- Animal with 4 legs
- Says ROAR
- Has a mane

Topic: Bird
- Animal with wings
- Lays eggs
- Lives in a nest

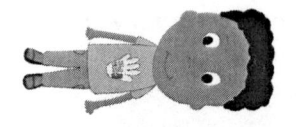

Purchasers of *Conversation Club* are granted permission to print materials from the *Instructor Manual* and *Storybooks* at www.aapcpublishing.net/ccdw. None of the handouts may be reproduced to generate revenue for any program or individual. Unauthorized use beyond this privilege is prosecutable under federal law.

Unit 2, Activity 2 Materials:
"What is a Topic?" Game Page 2 of 3

Topic: Playground
- Has swings
- Kids play on it
- Go down a slide

Topic: Zebra
- Animal with 4 legs
- Black and white stripes
- Eats grass

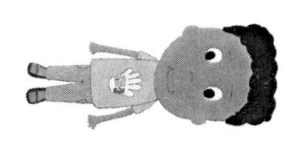

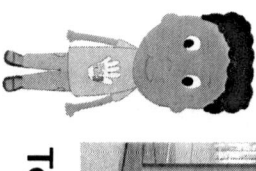

Topic: Fish
- Lives in water
- Has gills to breathe
- Has a tail and fins

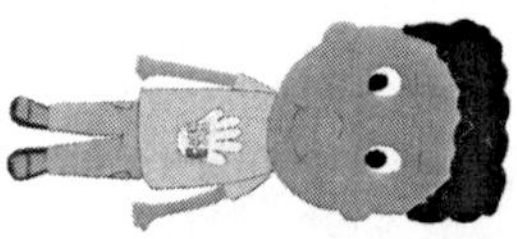

Topic: Giraffe
- Animal with long neck
- Has spots
- Eats leaves

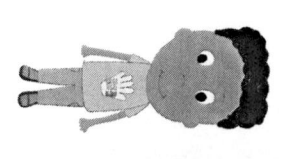

Unit 2: Selecting and Staying on Topic | 45

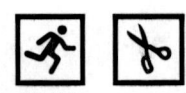

Unit 2, Activity 2 Materials:
"What is a Topic?" Game Page 3 of 3

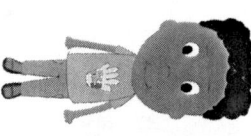

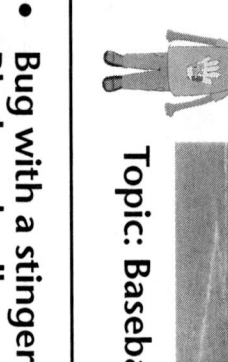

Topic: Baseball
- Game with 4 bases
- Hit the ball
- Three outs

Topic: Bee
- Bug with a stinger
- Black and yellow
- Makes honey

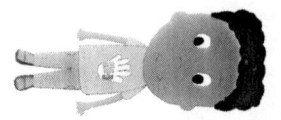

Topic: Swimming
- Wear a bathing suit
- Can be inside or outside
- Get wet

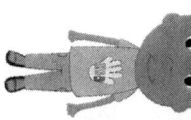

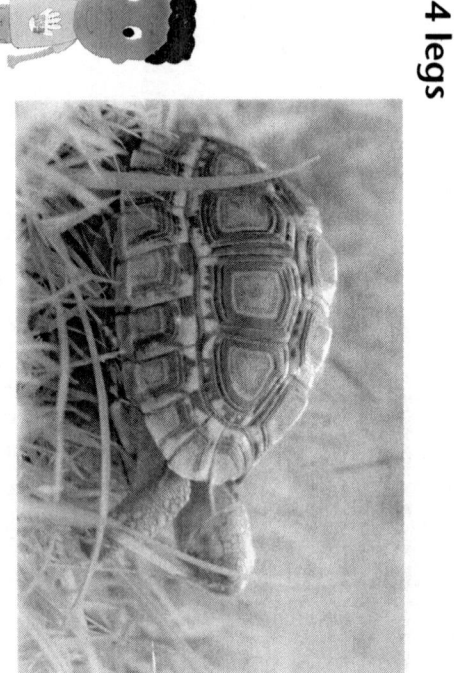

Topic: Turtles
- Animal with a shell
- Can swim in water
- 4 legs

46 | Conversation Club

**Unit 2, Activity 3 Materials:
"What is a Topic?" Game**

Unit 2, Activity 4 Materials:
"What is a Topic?" Game Topic Cards Page 1 of 5

Topic Cards

Unit 2 — Topic

Card Game

Topic Cards

Unit 2, Activity 4 Materials:
"What is a Topic?" Game Topic Cards

Where do you live?	Do you have any pets? What are their names?
Do you have brothers and sisters? What are their names?	What do you do when you go home?

Unit 2: Selecting and Staying on Topic

Unit 2, Activity 4 Materials:
"What is a Topic?" Game Topic Cards Page 3 of 5

What is your favorite holiday?

What is your middle name?

Hello my name is
Freddy **Joseph** Foster

What is your favorite food?

What TV show do you watch?

Unit 2, Activity 4 Materials:
"What is a Topic?" Game Topic Cards Page 4 of 5

What movie do you like?	What video games do you play?
What do you do on the weekend?	How old are you?

Unit 2: Selecting and Staying on Topic | 51

Unit 2, Activity 4 Materials:
"What is a Topic?" Game Topic Cards Page 5 of 5

What is your favorite book?	What do you play at recess?
Who is in your family?	What is your favorite subject in school? P.E. Music Art

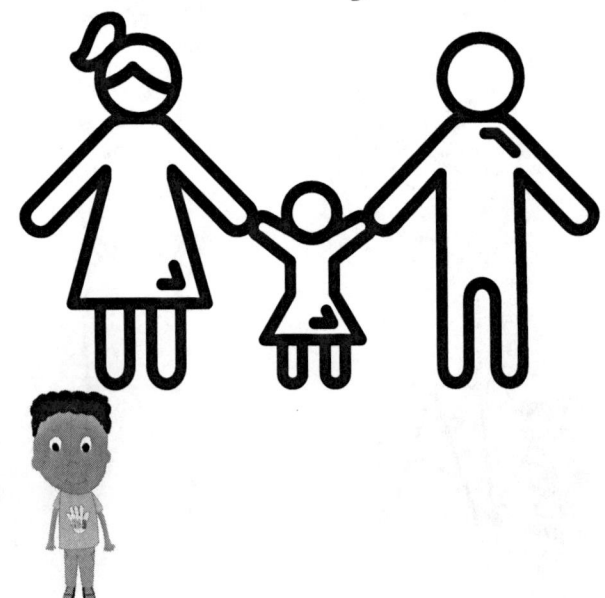

52 | Conversation Club

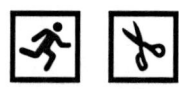

Unit 2, Activity 5 Materials:
Super Brainstorm #1

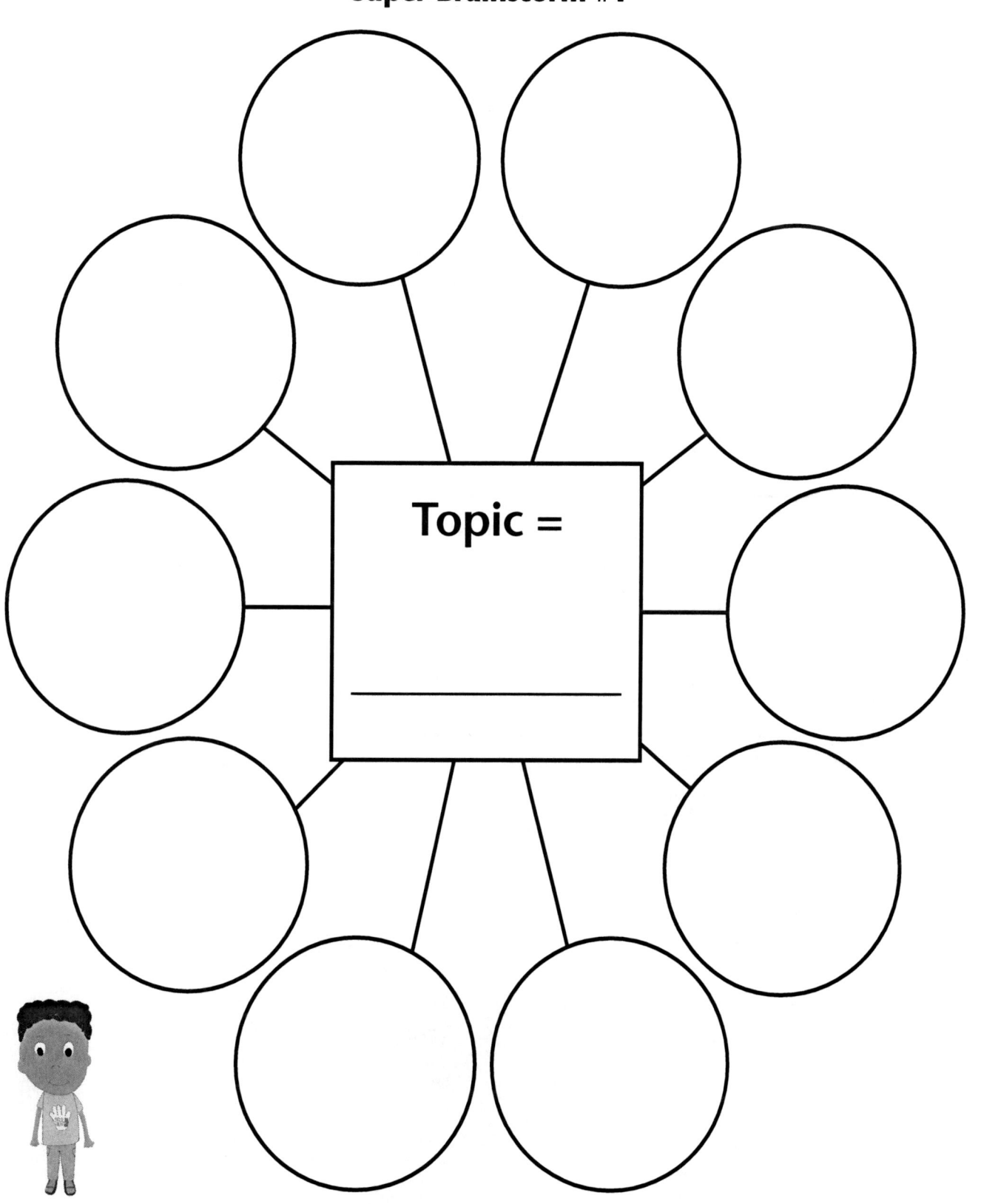

Topic =
_____

Unit 2: Selecting and Staying on Topic | 53

**Unit 2, Activity 5 Materials:
Super Brainstorm #2**

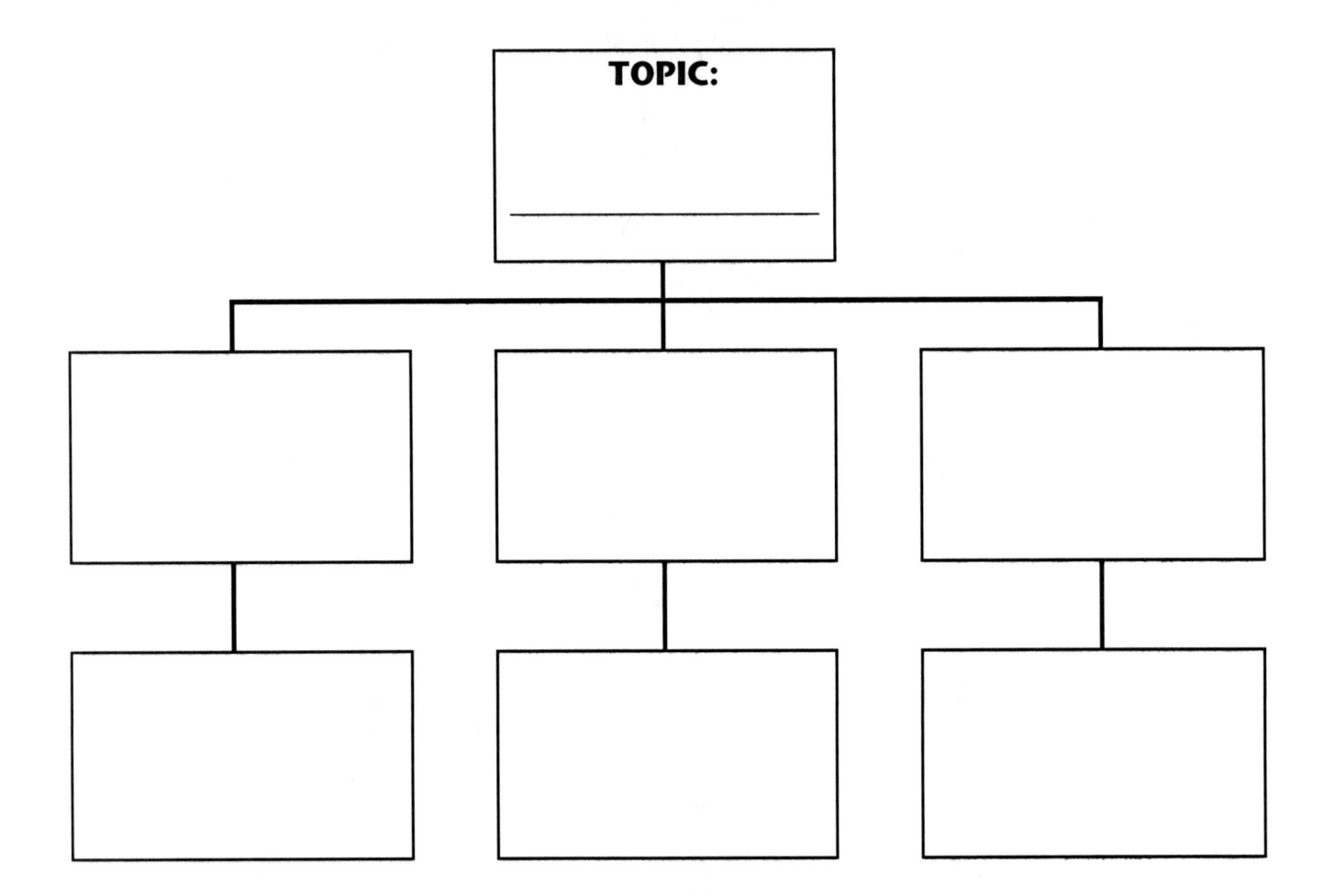

TOPIC:
_____

54 | Conversation Club

Unit 2, Activity 6 Materials: Conversation Club Files

Conversation Club File

Name:

Favorite TV show:
_____

Favorite sport:
_____

Favorite food:
_____

Where do you live?
_____

Who is in your family?
_____

What do you like to do after school?
_____
_____
_____
_____

Unit 2: Reinforcement Page

Name:	Name:	Name:
Share Space	Share Space	Share Space
Answer Questions	Answer Questions	Answer Questions
Ask Questions	Ask Questions	Ask Questions
Topic	Topic	Topic

Unit 3: Keeping the Conversation Going

What Will Club Members Learn?

In this unit, club members will meet Friendly Freddy's best friend, Paco the Parrot. They will learn Paco's favorite words: *who, what, where, when* and *why* (*WH* words). Club members will have many opportunities to practice asking and answering *WH* questions, and will use a graphic organizer to generate descriptive statements that include information related to each *WH* word.

Why Do We Teach This?

Children with social cognitive deficits may offer brief statements but be unable to elaborate. In addition, their statements may be left hanging without any follow-up from peers. Learning the *WH* questions not only helps club members keep the conversation going by providing a structure for asking questions, it also helps them learn to think about the gestalt, or "big picture," related to the topic of discussion, instead of focusing on an isolated detail about a topic. Paco teaches club members the meaning of each *WH* word. He teaches them strategies to elicit more information by analyzing their conversation partner's statement and asking *WH* questions to complete their understanding of the concept. The goal of this unit is to provide club members with a structure for asking and answering questions about a given topic, thereby increasing the number of details shared about a given topic.

Outcome Objectives

This unit teaches club members to do the following:

- Ask and answer a *what* question
- Ask and answer a *where* question
- Ask and answer a *when* question
- Ask and answer a *who* question
- Ask and answer a *why* question
- Create a descriptive statement that includes *what, where, when,* and *who* information
- Use a graphic organizer to recall descriptive statements including *what, where, when,* and *who* information

✓ Reinforcement

Provide one point each time club members:

- Share space by sitting or standing at an appropriate distance
- Ask on-topic *WH* questions
- Answer on-topic questions

Activity List

1. *Storybooks:* "Interesting Conversations Using *WH* Words"
2. *WH* Words Game
3. "Where Are They?" Game
4. Barrier Game
5. Meet Paco the Parrot! – Complete Comments: Part 1
6. Meet Paco the Parrot! – Complete Comments: Part 2

Activities

Activity 1: "Interesting Questions Using *WH* Words" Story

Summary

The purpose of the story is to introduce club members to Friendly Freddy's best friend, Paco the Parrot, and to learn about Paco's favorite words: *who, what, where, when, and why* (*WH* words). Club members learn how to ask and answer questions using *WH* words. This will help club members expand their knowledge around a topic, make their exchanges more interesting and meaningful, and keep conversation going.

Materials

- *Storybooks:* "Interesting Questions Using *WH* Words"
- Unit 3 Reinforcement Page

Talking Points for Instructor:

"Friendly Freddy and the Conversation Club are back again, and we've got another problem in the clubhouse. Club members have figured out what topics they can talk about, but their conversations are not very interesting, and no one is having any fun! Someone is going to have to save the day and make the club conversation more fun and interesting."

Club Agenda

1. Have club members recite the password.
2. Review: What is a topic? Name four topics you like to talk about. What is one reason you have a conversation with someone?
3. Introduce activity.
4. Read "Interesting Questions Using *WH* Words."
5. Add club members' points.
6. Wrap up.

Language to Support Learning

"That is a good 'who' question, because it made me think about the people who were there."

"We don't know the place where the accident happened. Let's ask a 'where' question to help us find out."

Unit 3: Keeping the Conversation Going | 59

Activity 2: WH Words Game

Summary

Paco the Parrot reviews his favorite words in this lesson – *who, what, where, when* and *why* (*WH* words). Club members practice generating *WH* questions about a given topic/picture.

Materials

- *WH* Words Game Picture Cards, pages 1–2 (cut ahead of time)
- *WH* Word Game Word Cards, pages 1–2 (cut ahead of time)
- Unit 3 Reinforcement Page

Set-up

Instructor places the Picture Cards in one pile and *WH* word cards in a separate pile.

Activity Rules

1. Player 1 selects a picture card and shows it to Player 2 (e.g., a picture of food).
2. Player 2 selects a *WH* Word Card and generates a question about the topic using that word (e.g., WHAT: *"What do you like to eat for dinner?"* WHEN: *"When do you like to eat dinner?"*).
3. Players take turns selecting *WH* cards and generating questions.
4. If a player selects a wild card, they can choose whatever *WH* word they want.
5. Club members will earn points for asking and answering on-topic questions. Club members will also earn points for positioning themselves correctly to have a conversation.

Talking Points for Instructor:

"Paco the Parrot is super excited. Today, Paco tells us his favorite words. Not only are these his favorite words, but these words help all of the other club members have more interesting conversations, share more easily, and learn more information. We are going to ask questions using these words. Club members, you will earn points for asking WH questions and answering questions on topic."

Club Agenda

1. Have club members recite the password.
2. Review: Who is Paco the Parrot? What are Paco's favorite words? Why does he want us to use the *WH* words in our conversations?
3. Reread "Interesting Questions Using *WH* Words" (optional).
4. Introduce activity.
5. Play game.
6. Add club members' points.
7. Wrap up.

Language to Support Learning

"That is a great on-topic question."

"I have learned so much interesting information because you have asked all of the 'WH' questions."

Activity 3: "Where Are They?" Game

Summary

This game is designed to give club members an opportunity to practice asking and answering *WH* questions and reinforce the idea that conversations help us share and learn information.

Materials

- "Where Are They?" Game Cards (cut ahead of time)
- *WH* Word Game Word Cards (from Activity 2)
- Unit 3
- Reinforcement Page

Set-up

Place "Where Are They?" Game Cards face down in a pile. Place *WH* Word Cards face down in a separate pile.

Activity Rules

1. Player 1 looks at a picture of a familiar scene (e.g., a zoo) and does not show the picture to Player 2.
2. Player 2 asks *WH* questions to find out key details about the picture (e.g., Q: "Who is there?" A: "*Parents and kids*" or Q: "What are they doing?" A: "*Looking at animals*").
3. When Player 2 correctly guesses the picture, he selects the next card, and play continues.
4. Club members will earn points for asking and answering on-topic questions.

Talking Points for Instructor:

"The object of this game is to guess what your partner is looking at on his card. You will use Paco's favorite words to ask questions and get clues about the picture your partner is looking at. Use your partner's clues to help you make a picture in your mind of what they are describing. Once you think you know what your partner is looking at, you can guess. Club members, you will earn points for asking 'WH' questions and answering on-topic questions."

Club Agenda

1. Have club members recite the password.
2. Review: What are Paco's favorite words? Who can remember two topics we talked about last time we met? Who can remember a fact they learned about a club member during our last conversation?
3. Reread "Interesting Questions Using *WH* Words" (optional).
4. Introduce activity.
5. Play game.
6. Add club members' points.
7. Wrap up.

Language to Support Learning

"I liked that 'what' question. It helped you learn more about what the people in the picture are doing."

"That was a good 'when' question. It helped you learn more about the time of day."

"I can tell you are thinking about what your partner said and making a picture of it in your mind."

Unit 3: Keeping the Conversation Going | 61

Activity 4: Barrier Game

Summary

This game is designed to provide club members with additional practice asking and answering *WH* questions, while reinforcing the use of conversation to share and learn information. One club member builds a picture and keeps it hidden from other club members. Other club members then ask *WH* questions to gather clues to help them arrange their own pictures to look like the original.

Materials

- Barrier Game Location Board
- Barrier Game Icons (cut in advance)
- *WH* Word Cards from Activity 2 (optional)
- Unit 3 Reinforcement Page

Set-up

Two players sit across from each other. Each player receives one location board and one set of icons. Make sure players cannot see each other's Location Boards.

Activity Rules

1. Player 1 puts two icons in each quadrant of the Location Board.

2. When Player 1 is finished placing icons on the hidden Location Board, Player 2 asks Player 1 *WH* questions to find out where he placed his icons (e.g., Q: "Who is on the playground?" A: "*Tiger.*" Q: "What is Tiger doing?" A: "*Sliding.*" Q: "Where is Tiger sliding?" A: "*On the green slide*"). Based on the answers, Player 2 should try to make her board look like Player 1's board.

3. Once Player 2 has placed all of her pieces, both players reveal their boards and see if they match.

4. Club members will earn points for asking and answering questions, and "checking in" with their eyes.

Talking Points for Instructor:

"Paco the Parrot wants us to use his favorite words to uncover clues. These clues will help you make a picture that looks exactly like the one your partner builds. Your partner is going to create a picture, but he is not going to show you the picture. Ask WH questions to find out what his picture looks like. When you think you've figured it out, we can check to see if the pictures are the same. Club members, you will earn points for asking WH questions and answering your partner's questions."

Club Agenda

1. Have club members recite the password.
2. Review: Who are the club members we have met so far? What are Paco the Parrot's favorite words? Why do we use these words in a conversation?
3. Reread "Interesting Questions Using WH Words" (optional).
4. Introduce activity.
5. Play game.
6. Add club members' points.
7. Wrap up.

Language to Support Learning

"I could tell you were thinking about your partner, because you were looking at her."

"That WH question just gave you a lot of good information."

Activity 5: Meet Paco the Parrot!
Complete Comments: Part 1

Summary

In this activity, Paco the Parrot helps club members use his favorite words to create complete, descriptive statements. A complete statement includes information that answers each of the *WH* words. A descriptive statement will use the *WH* words to share information that describes something. Complete, descriptive statements do both. Club members focus on generating descriptive statements that other club members will find interesting. As club members listen to the descriptive statements, they will use a Paco the Parrot graphic organizer to focus on what information they know, and what information is missing. This will help them determine if the statement is complete. Each part of Paco's body represents a *WH* word that must be answered in the statement.

Materials

- Laminated Paco image and *WH* word body parts. *Note:* Attach Velcro to the back of each part
- Meet Paco the Parrot!
- Complete Comments: Part 1 sentence strips (cut)
- Unit 3 Reinforcement Page

Set-up

Place the body of Paco the Parrot, fully assembled, in the middle of the table. Place sentence strips in a pile beside Paco.

Activity Rules

1. Remove the *WH* words from Paco's body and place them on the table.
2. Player 1 selects a sentence strip and reads it aloud (e.g., "*Julie went to the toy store on Monday to buy a stuffed animal*").
3. The instructor picks up one *WH* word (a piece of Paco's body). The instructor asks a *WH* question using the word, and club members answer (e.g., WHO – Q: "Do we know who did it?" A: "*Julie.*" WHAT – Q: "Do we know what happened?" A: "*Julie bought a stuffed animal*"). As players answer *WH* questions, they stick the related *WH* word back on Paco's body.
4. Game is over when club members have completely replaced all of Paco's body parts.
5. Club members will earn points for asking and answering questions.

Talking Points for Instructor:

"We all remember that Paco the Parrot has five favorite words: who, what, where, when, and why. We use them to ask and answer questions. These words help us find out more information and keep our conversations going. When we ask club members questions, it lets them know we are thinking about them and are interested, or want to know more information about them. For example, if I am thinking about all of you, and I am interested in knowing your favorite colors, I would use Paco's favorite word, 'what,' and ask, 'What is your favorite color?' Club members, you will earn points for asking and answering 'WH' questions. Don't forget to 'check in' with your eyes when you are talking."

Club Agenda

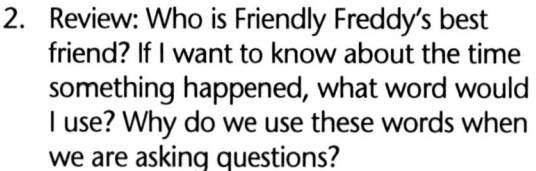

1. Have club members recite the password.
2. Review: Who is Friendly Freddy's best friend? If I want to know about the time something happened, what word would I use? Why do we use these words when we are asking questions?
3. Reread "Interesting Questions Using *WH* Words" (optional).
4. Introduce activity.
5. Do activity.
6. Add club members' points.
7. Wrap up.

Language to Support Learning

"You identified 'what' happened."

"You listened for the time information to tell us 'when' the game happened."

"I can tell you were thinking about what the club member said, because you answered all of the WH *questions."*

Activity 6: Meet Paco the Parrot!
Complete Comments: Part 2

Summary

In this activity, club members reinforce and practice skills from the previous activity. Club members will have the opportunity to generate sentences on their own. Partners (with the help of the instructor) will build Paco's body as they reflect on what they hear.

Materials

- Laminated Paco image and *WH* word body parts with Velcro attached to the back of each part
- Unit 3 Reinforcement Page

Set-up

Place Paco the Parrot, with his body assembled, in the middle of the table.

Activity Rules

1. Remove the *WH* words from Paco's body and place them on the table.
2. Club members take turns making a statement about real or imagined events (e.g., "*Billy went to the park to play on Friday*").
3. Remaining club members pick up each *WH* word, ask and answer information about the *WH* word, and add pieces to Paco's body (e.g., WHO – Q: "Do we know who did it? A: "*Billy.*" WHAT – Q: "Do we know what happened?" A: "*Billy played at the park*").
4. Game is over when club members completely replace all of Paco's parts.
5. Club members will earn points for asking and answering questions.

Talking Points for Instructor:

"Remember building Paco's body during our last activity? In this activity, you get to put a body part on Paco for every one of his favorite words you use. Now it is your turn to come up with a sentence and the other club members will build Paco's body based on what you say. Don't forget — you will earn points for asking questions, answering questions, and making sure your body is in the right position when you are having a conversation."

Club Agenda

1. Have club members recite the password.
2. Review: Who is Paco? What does he help us do? Why is it important to make complete comments?
3. Reread "Interesting Questions Using *WH* Words" (optional).
4. Introduce activity.
5. Do activity.
6. Add club members' points.
7. Wrap up.

Language to Support Learning

"*That was a really complete and interesting statement. I'd love to know more about that!*"

"*You told me about 'who,' 'where,' and 'when.' I am interested in 'what.'*"

Generalization Opportunities

When a club member shares information with you, respond by highlighting the specific information they shared.

Shared information: *"Ms. Jonna, I went to the store with my mom yesterday."* Response: *"Thanks for telling me where you went, who you went with, and when you went. Can you tell me how you got there?"*

Highlight when their communication, conversation, or behavior has made someone feel good or given them good thoughts: *"We all loved hearing about your weekend. You gave us good thoughts and good information. I would really like to keep talking to you."*

Help them recall and process what they have just heard using the *WH* words as prompts: å*"In the book, we just learned all about Johnny. What did we learn Johnny likes to do? Where does Johnny like to go? Who was he hanging out with?"*

If club members are having a difficult time with one or more goals, you might want to consider:

- Repeating an activity
- Modifying an existing activity
- Writing *WH* words on a sheet of paper as a visual reference for club members who are having difficulty remembering them
- Challenging club members who are having difficulty using one or more of the *WH* words to list them all and cross each one off as it is used
- Excluding the question word *why* for children that have difficulty with higher-order thinking, since *why* is the most difficult of the *WH* words

Materials

**Unit 3, Activity 2 Materials:
WH Words Game Word Cards**

WHO	WHAT	WHERE
WHEN	WHY	

Purchasers of *Conversation Club* are granted permission to print materials from the *Instructor Manual* and *Storybooks* at www.aapcpublishing.net/ccdw. None of the handouts may be reproduced to generate revenue for any program or individual. Unauthorized use beyond this privilege is prosecutable under federal law.

Unit 3, Activity 2 Materials:
WH Words Game Picture Cards

Unit 3: Keeping the Conversation Going | 69

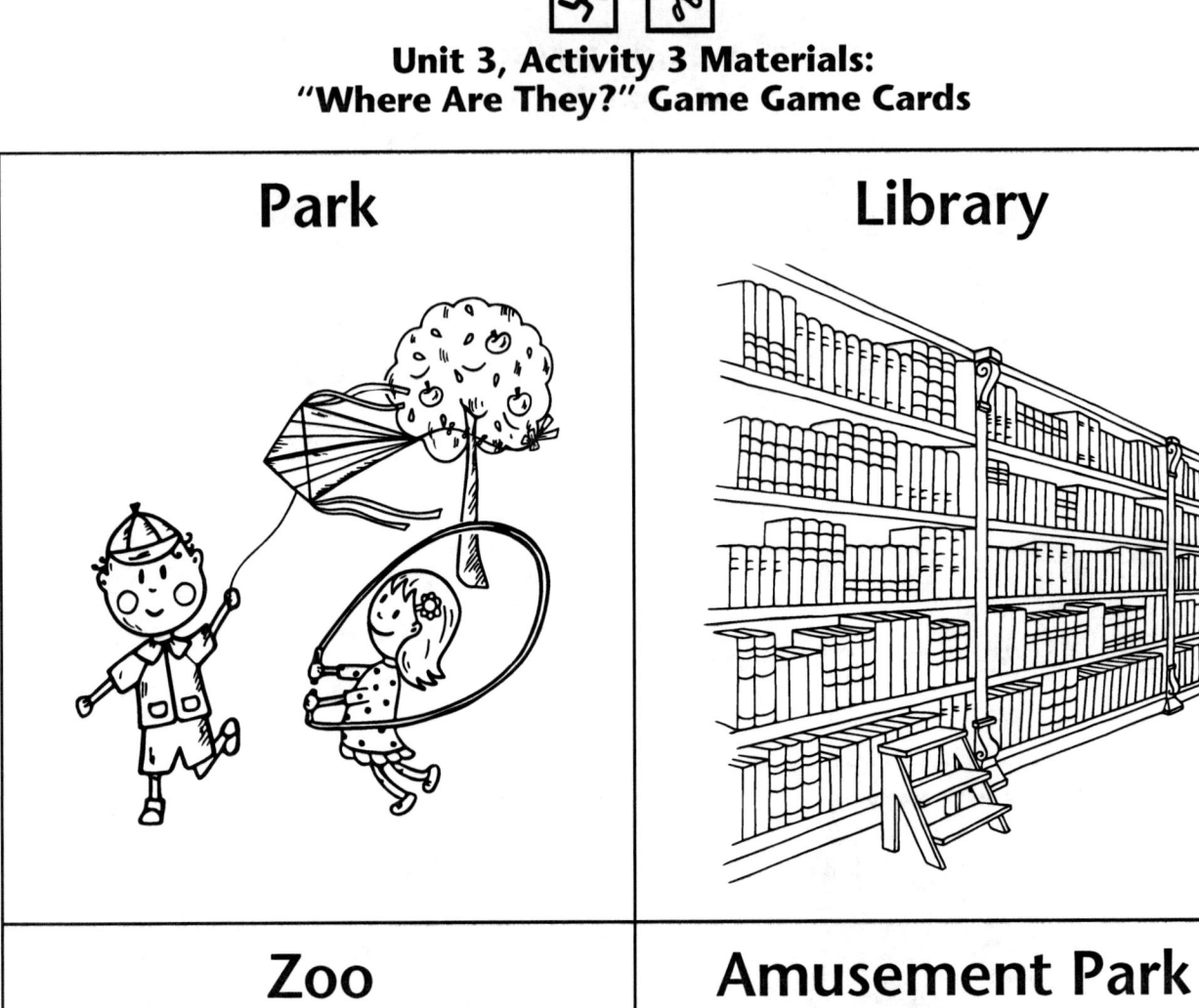

Unit 3, Activity 3 Materials:
"Where Are They?" Game Game Cards

Park

Library

Zoo

Amusement Park

70 | Conversation Club

Unit 3, Activity 4 Materials:
Barrier Game Location Board

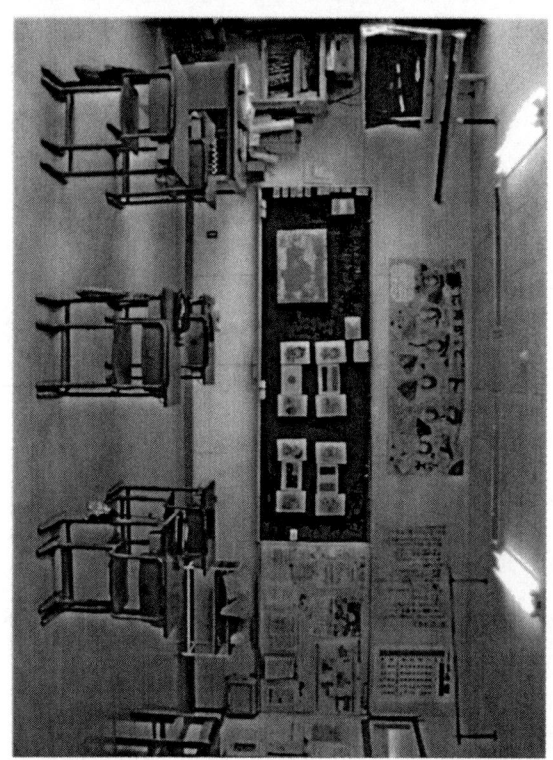

Unit 3: Keeping the Conversation Going | 71

**Unit 3, Activity 4 Materials:
Barrier Game Icons**

72 | Conversation Club

Unit 3, Activity 5 Materials:
Meet Paco the Parrot! Complete Comments: Part 1

Ben went to the park to play on the slide yesterday.

Next week, Ethan is going to Florida to visit his grandmother.

In the winter, Sam will go sledding in the park with his brother.

Juan is going to dinner at the pizza restaurant on Thursday.

Louis went to math class at 11:00 a.m. in Ms. Brady's classroom.

Maria played tag in the gym yesterday.

Mary swam in the pool last summer.

David jumped on the bed in his room last night.

**Unit 3, Activity 5 & 6 Materials:
Meet Paco the Parrot! Complete Comments: Part 1 & 2**

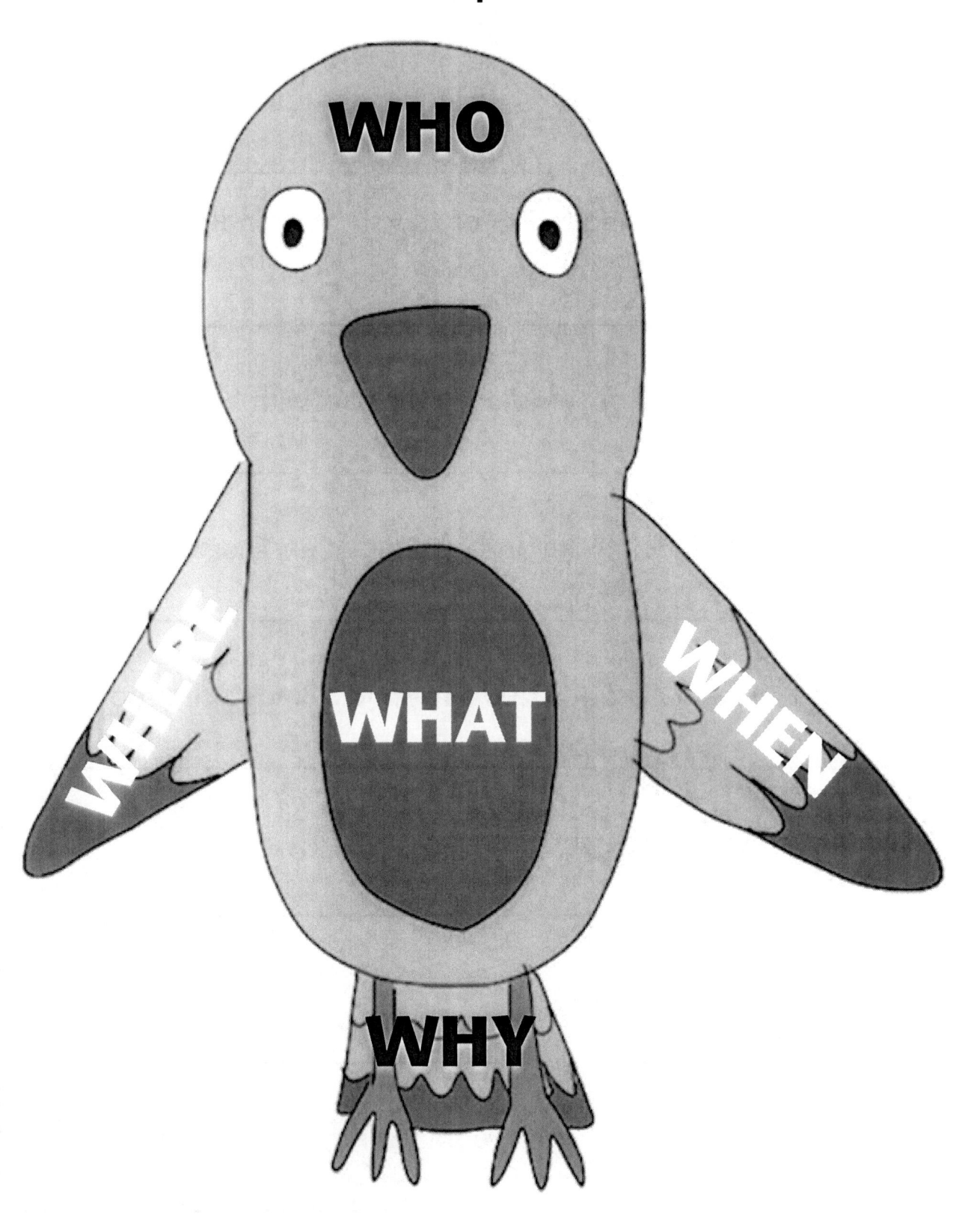

74 | Conversation Club

✓ Unit 3: Reinforcement Page

Name:	Name:	Name:
Share Space	Share Space	Share Space
Answer Questions ?	Answer Questions ?	Answer Questions ?
Ask *WH* Questions	Ask *WH* Questions	Ask *WH* Questions

Unit 3: Keeping the Conversation Going | 75

Unit 4:

Using Our Eyes and Ears to Think about Our Conversation Partner

What Will Club Members Learn?

In this unit, club members will be introduced to the twins, Listening Lisa and Looking Louie. Listening Lisa helps us listen to what our conversation partner says. She helps us identify important information, or "key words." We are then able to use "key words" to ask follow-up questions. Listening Lisa also helps us make sure we have our conversation partner's attention and teaches us attention-gaining strategies, like using our partner's name. Looking Louie reminds us that in order to make sure our conversation partner is ready to listen, we first need to make eye contact with our conversation partner, or "check in" with our eyes. Club members will learn that when you look and listen, people will want to keep having conversations with you.

Why Do We Teach This?

The core goals of this unit are to teach club members how to identify and use the main idea to develop follow-up questions, and to learn strategies for ensuring that we have the attention of our conversation partners. Children with social cognition deficits often have difficulty initiating and continuing a conversation. They may not acknowledge the information that has been shared with them, and may change the topic abruptly or fail to respond. Additionally, they may begin talking without having the attention of their partners. Club members will learn that using follow-up questions or statements will help their conversation partners feel that they are being listened to. Strategies for gaining attention will help the club members make sure that their partners are ready to listen.

Outcome Objectives

This unit teaches club members to do the following:

- Identify a key word in a statement
- Use the key word in a follow-up question/comment
- Use eyes to "check in" with conversation partner
- Identify whether or not conversation partner is paying attention
- Use attention-gaining behaviors to gain conversation partner's attention (e.g., saying partner's name or tapping partner on the shoulder)

Reinforcement

Provide one point each time club members:

- Gain partner's attention
- "Check in" with their eyes
- Ask on-topic *WH* questions
- Answer on-topic questions

Activity List

1. *Storybooks:* "Listening and Looking, Part One" (Listening Lisa)
2. Key Words with Conversation Tracker
3. *Storybooks*: "Listening and Looking, Part Two" (Looking Louie)
4. "Checking in" with Our Eyes Game
5. Gaining Our Partner's Attention Game

Activities

Activity 1: "Listening and Looking – Part One"

Summary

The Conversation Club members take a trip to the zoo. Listening Lisa helps Friendly Freddy identify key words so that he can ask Paco follow-up questions and continue the conversation. Using key words will help club members show their conversation partners that they are listening to them.

Materials

- *Storybooks:* "Listening and Looking – Part One"
- Unit 4 Reinforcement Page

Talking Points for Instructor:

"Today is a big day! We are going to meet the third member of the Conversation Club, Listening Lisa. She's going to teach us a new club rule, and new ways to earn points. She helps us be good listeners when we are having conversations. We have to be good listeners so we know what other club members are talking about, and so they will want to be around us and spend more time with us. Club members, you will earn points for gaining your partner's attention, 'checking in' with your eyes, answering questions, and asking on-topic WH questions.

Club Agenda

1. Have club members recite the password.
2. Review: What are two of Paco's favorite words? How does your conversation partner know that you are ready to talk? What is one reason why conversations are important?
3. Introduce activity.
4. Read the first part of the "Listening and Looking" story, and stop at identified points throughout the story to gauge club members' understanding. After reading the story, have club members select a topic and do a quick brainstorm about the topic (see Unit 2: Activity 5 for an example of the brainstorm).
5. Add club members' points.
6. Wrap up.

Language to Support Learning

"Great job coming up with key words that have to do with our topic. I can tell you are paying attention."

Unit 4: Using Our Eyes and Ears to Think about Our Conversation Partner | 79

Activity 2: Key Words with Conversation Tracker

Summary

In this lesson, Listening Lisa helps club members listen to what their conversation partners are saying by identifying key words and using the Conversation Tracker. The key word in a statement is the "main idea" and tells us what the statement is about. Clueing in on the key word or identifying the main idea helps club members generate follow-up statements and questions. The Conversation Tracker offers a way to record the key words found within each statement or question. Club members can use the chart to visually track the flow of conversation.

Materials

- Key Words with Conversation Tracker and directions
- Unit 4 Reinforcement Page

Set-up

Print Key Words with Conversation Tracker in advance.

Talking Points for Instructor:

"Remember meeting Listening Lisa? She wants us to be good listeners when we are having conversations with our conversation partners. She wants us to listen for key words and then use the key word to ask questions or make comments. A key word tells us what the question or comment is about. For example, Lisa said, 'I went swimming.' Ask yourself, 'What did Lisa do?' The key word is 'swimming.' To keep the conversation going, ask her a question about swimming. Use a WH word. For example, 'Where did you go swimming?' If we are good listeners, we will learn new information about our partners, and they will know we are interested in them. They will want to keep having conversations with us! Don't forget — you will earn points for gaining your partner's attention, 'checking in' with your eyes, answering questions, and asking on-topic WH questions."

Club Agenda

1. Have club members recite the password.
2. Review: Who is Paco Parrot? Why does Friendly Freddy want us to have conversations?
3. Reread "Listening and Looking – Part 1" (optional).
4. Introduce activity.
5. Do activity.
6. Add club members' points.
7. Wrap up.

80 | Conversation Club

Activity Rules

1. Players identify a topic (e.g., soccer) and instructor writes it in the *Topic* box of the chart. (Topic Cards can also be used to identify a topic for this activity.)
2. Player 1 asks a question that includes both a *WH* word and the key word that is in the *Topic* box of the chart. The instructor writes the question in the *Question* box of the chart.
3. Player 2 answers the question, and the instructor writes the new key word in the next *Key Word* box.
4. Players take turns selecting *WH* cards and generating questions until the chart is complete, with players asking and answering questions and the instructor writing the questions and key words in the boxes.
5. Club members will earn points for gaining their partners' attention, "checking in" with their eyes, answering questions, and asking on-topic *WH* questions.

Example

Player 1: "Where did you play soccer?" (Instructor writes question in the *Question* box.)

Player 2: "I played in McLean." (Instructor writes the key word, *McLean,* in the *Key Word* box.)

Player 1: "Who did you play with in McLean?" (Instructor writes question in the *Question* box.)

Player 2: "I played with my soccer team." (Instructor writes *soccer team* in the *Key Word* box.)

Player 1: "When will you play with your soccer team again?" (Instructor writes question in the *Question* box.)

Player 2: "I will play with them on Saturday." (Instructor writes *Saturday* in the *Key Word* box.)

Topic : *Soccer*

WH Question	Key Word
Where did you play *soccer*?	*McLean*
Who did you play with in *McLean*?	*My soccer team*
When will you play with your *soccer* team again?	*Saturday*
What else will you do on *Saturday*?	*Go to the movies*

Language to Support Learning

"Great job using the key word in your question. I can tell you were really listening."

"The key word in Evan's sentence is soccer. *Can you ask a* WH *question about soccer?"*

"Brendan just told you that he went to a baseball game. I wonder who he went with. How could you find out?"

Unit 4: Using Our Eyes and Ears to Think about Our Conversation Partner | 81

Activity 3: "Listening and Looking – Part Two"

Summary

The purpose of this lesson is to learn strategies for gaining the attention of a conversation partner to make sure that they are ready to listen.

Materials

- *Storybooks:* "Listening and Looking – Part Two"
- Unit 4 Reinforcement Page

Talking Points for Instructor:

"Today is another big day. We are going to meet the fourth member of the Conversation Club. He's going to teach us a new clubhouse rule, and a new way to earn points. Let's meet Looking Louie. Looking Louie helps us use our eyes to be good listeners. When we 'check in' with our eyes during a conversation, our conversation partners know that we are listening, and it makes them feel important. Our conversation partners will want to have more conversations with us if they know that we are paying attention to them. Club members, you will earn points for gaining your partners' attention, 'checking in' with your eyes, answering questions, and asking on-topic WH questions."

Club Agenda

1. Have club members recite the password.
2. Review: Name two club members. What topic did Lisa teach us about? How do you find the key words in a sentence?
3. Introduce activity.
4. Read the second part of the "Listening and Looking" story from *Storybooks*, and stop at identified points throughout the story to gauge club members' understanding. After reading the story, have club members select a topic and do a quick instructor-led brainstorm about the topic (see Unit 2: Activity 5, for brainstorm templates and an example).
5. Add club members' points.
6. Wrap up.

Language to Support Learning

"When you called Evan by his name before talking to him, he knew you wanted his attention."

"I like the way you got Brendan's attention before you asked him if he wanted to play."

Activity 4: "Checking in" with Our Eyes Game

Summary

In this lesson, club members will learn that Looking Louie's goal is for everyone to have their eyes on their conversation partners. When we "check in" with our eyes, it shows that we are thinking about our conversation partners. "Checking in" with our eyes also helps us make sure our conversation partner is paying attention and is interested in the conversation.

Materials

- Category Cards (cut out in advance)
- Dry erase board and marker
- Unit 4 Reinforcement Page

Set-up

Place a white board in view of the club members, and stack the Category Cards on the table.

Activity Rules

1. Instructor draws a Category Card and writes the name of the category on the white board. If the category is *numbers* or *the alphabet,* ask players to say their answers in order (i.e., "one, two, three," or "A, B, C").
2. Players set a goal (e.g., "Let's count to 20 and only use our eyes to tell our partner that it is his turn").
3. Player 1 identifies the first word in the category (e.g., "one"). Player 1 then looks at Player 2 to let Player 2 know that it is her turn.
4. Player 2 identifies a second item in the category (e.g., "two"), and so on.
5. Instructor picks a new Category Card when players have no more ideas for the original category.
6. Club members will earn points each time they use their eyes to notify their conversation partners that it is their turn.

Talking Points for Instructor:

"Friendly Freddy is so excited for you to meet Looking Louie. Looking Louie wants us to use our eyes to look at our conversation partners when having a conversation. When we use our eyes to look at our conversation partners, they know we are listening to them. Today, we will practice looking at our partner when we are talking.

You can earn points when you get your partner's attention, "check in" with your eyes, answer questions, and ask on-topic WH questions."

Club Agenda

1. Have club members recite the password.
2. Review: What is one rule of the Conversation Club? What does Listening Lisa want us to listen for? How do you get ready for a conversation?
3. Reread "Listening and Looking"
4. Introduce activity.
5. Play game.
6. Add club members' points.
7. Wrap up.

Language to Support Learning

"I really liked how you used your eyes to look at me when you told me about the party."

"I could tell you were thinking about me because you used your eyes to look at me."

84 | Conversation Club

Activity 5: Gaining Our Partner's Attention Games

Summary

In this lesson, club members will be challenged to combine the skills learned from Listening Lisa and Looking Louie. By "checking in" with their eyes, club members will determine if their conversation partners are listening; this also shows that they are thinking about others. Club members will learn strategies to regain attention when their partners are not listening or showing interest.

Materials

- Foam ball or squishy ball
- Question Cards (cut out in advance)
- Dry erase board and marker
- Unit 4 Reinforcement Page

Set-up

Provide players with a foam or squishy ball as they sit around a table. Place Question Cards on the table.

Activity Rules

Game #1

1. Player 1 passes the squishy ball to another player, being sure to "check in" with her eyes and use the name of the player she is passing to.
2. Game continues until all players have had several turns.

Game #2

1. Player 1 engages with a distractor (e.g., squishy ball) or pretends to be distracted.
2. Player 2 picks a Question Card.
3. Player 2 uses strategies learned from the story to get Player 1's attention before asking the question.
4. Reverse roles and repeat.
5. Club members will earn points for gaining their partner's attention, "checking in" with their eyes, answering questions, and asking on-topic *WH* questions.

Talking Points for Instructor:

"Listening Lisa and Looking Louie want to see what you have learned. Are you ready for a challenge? We're going to see if you can use what Lisa and Louie have taught you to make sure that you are on your toes and really listening. We are each going to have a turn getting each other's attention and asking a question."

Club Agenda

1. Have club members recite the password.
2. Review: What are Paco the Parrot's favorite words? How do we know our conversation partner is ready to listen?
3. Reread "Listening and Looking" (optional).
4. Introduce activity.
5. Play games.
6. Add club members' points.
7. Wrap up.

Language to Support Learning

"I really liked how you used Juan's name before asking your question."

"Looking Louie would be proud that you waited for Lucy to look at you before asking your question."

Generalization Opportunities

Point out when club members get their peers' attention before talking to them. At recess or during game play, encourage club members to practice attention-gaining strategies. At the end of a conversation, have club members identify key words from their peers' statements.

If club members are having a difficult time with one or more goals, you might want to consider:

- Repeating an activity
- Modifying an existing activity
- Seating members across from each other instead of next to each other to facilitate eye contact and body placement
- Showing videos or pictures to club members and asking them to determine if the subjects in the images are using good listening skills and "checking in" (making eye contact) appropriately
- Role playing skills taught in previous activities (e.g., tapping on their peer's shoulder or calling their partner's name) for club members who are having difficulty getting someone's attention

Materials

Unit 4, Activity 2 Materials:
Key Words with Conversation Tracker

Topic:	
WH Question	**Key Word**

Purchasers of *Conversation Club* are granted permission to print materials from the *Instructor Manual* and *Storybooks* at www.aapcpublishing.net/ccdw. None of the handouts may be reproduced to generate revenue for any program or individual. Unauthorized use beyond this privilege is prosecutable under federal law.

Unit 4, Activity 4 Materials:
"Checking in" with Our Eyes Game Category Cards

Numbers	Alphabet
1 2 3 4 5	A B C D E
Colors	**TV Shows**
Names (Hello my name is)	**Movies**
Choose your own ?	**Choose your own** ?

Unit 4: Using Our Eyes and Ears to Think about Our Conversation Partner | 89

Unit 4, Activity 5 Materials: Gaining Our Partner's Attention Games Question Cards

What do you like to do after school?	What books do you like?
What do you like to do on the playground?	Do you like to draw?
What movies do you like?	Do you like to play video games?
Who is your favorite *Conversation Club* character?	What is your favorite subject at school?
What do you like to do in the winter?	Do you like animals?
What is your favorite color?	Free Choice

Unit 4: Reinforcement Page

Name:	Name:	Name:
Gain Attention	Gain Attention	Gain Attention
"Check in" with Eyes	"Check in" with Eyes	"Check in" with Eyes
Answer Questions ?	Answer Questions ?	Answer Questions ?
Ask *WH* Questions	Ask *WH* Questions	Ask *WH* Questions

Unit 4: Using Our Eyes and Ears to Think about Our Conversation Partner

Unit 5: Conversation Repair

What Will Club Members Learn?

In this unit, club members will meet Fix It Farrah. Her main objective is to teach club members how to repair conversation breakdowns. Club members will participate in activities that focus on increasing their awareness when something goes wrong in the conversation. They will practice pinpointing problems and selecting strategies to repair breakdowns. Strategies include repeating the message, rephrasing the comment/question a different way, using a louder voice, regaining their conversation partner's attention, and shifting topics to a preferred topic of mutual interest. Fix It Farrah will help club members assess if a breakdown occurred because one conversation partner did not hear or did not understand. They will also find out how to assess their partner's nonverbal cues to determine if their peer is interested in what they are saying.

Why Do We Teach This?

The core goals of this unit are to help club members identify when a communication breakdown occurs, understand what caused the breakdown, and explore ways to repair the conversation. Even the most successful conversations have communication breakdowns, which require conversation partners to problem solve in the moment by using skills such as assessing nonverbal cues, metacognitive thinking, executive functioning, flexibility, and perspective taking. Children with social learning deficits often do not use or understand nonverbal communication skills to reference their conversation partners, check to see if their conversation partners are listening, or assess the level of interest their conversation partners show in the conversation. Even if they are verbally involved in the conversation, they may not be aware that their conversation partner is not listening or that a breakdown occurred. As a result, conversation may start and stop very frequently, or appear one-sided. By teaching club members what a conversation breakdown looks like, building their awareness of specific behaviors that cause a conversation breakdown, and teaching them strategies to repair the breakdown, they will be better prepared to fix problems on their own as they occur.

Outcome Objectives

This unit teaches club members to do the following:

- Identify if a conversation breakdown occurred
- Determine the cause of the conversation breakdown
- Select a strategy to repair the conversation breakdown

✓ Reinforcement

Provide one point each time club members:

- Use an indoor voice
- Check their space
- Ask on-topic *WH* questions
- Answer on-topic questions
- "Check in" with their eyes
- Use key words in a question or statement
- Gain a conversation partner's attention
- Remember information shared by a conversation partner
- Choose either a topic of shared interest or a partner's topic of interest

Activity List

1. *Storybooks:* "Let's Fix the Problem"
2. "Did Something Go Wrong?" Game, Part 1
3. "Did Something Go Wrong?" Game, Part 2
4. "Something Went Wrong. What Do I Do Now?" Game
5. "Fixing Problems in the Moment" Activity
6. "Are You Interested or Not?" Activity

Activities

Activity 1: "Let's Fix The Problem" Story

Summary

The purpose of the story is to introduce club members to Fix It Farrah. Feel free to reread this story as you move through the lessons in Unit 5. In "Let's Fix the Problem," club members will observe Farrah having conversations with club members. As she has conversations with the club members, situations arise in which the club members did not hear their conversation partners, were not listening, or did not understand. Fix It Farrah helps club members identify that something went wrong and shows them ways to fix the problem.

Materials

- *Storybooks:* "Let's Fix The Problem"
- Unit 5 Reinforcement Page

Talking Points for Instructor:

"Today, you are going to meet the fifth member of the Conversation Club, Fix It Farrah. Sometimes we have problems during conversations with our friends. Fix It Farrah helps us to fix those problems!"

Club Agenda

1. Have club members recite the password.
2. Review: Who is your favorite Conversation Club member? Why is it important to have conversations? What can you learn from a conversation?
3. Introduce activity.
4. Read "Let's Fix the Problem."
5. Add club members' points.
6. Wrap up.

Language to Support Learning

"Wow! You did a great job helping Fix It Farrah fix that problem and continue the conversation!"

"You are right! The problem was that she did not hear the person talking."

Unit 5: Conversation Repair | 95

Activity 2: "Did Something Go Wrong?" Game Part 1

Summary

Club members will identify when something goes wrong in the conversation and categorize the breakdown into one of three specified problems. The focus of this activity is the club members' self-awareness that they did not hear or understand information. Club members will listen to the instructor read sentences. The instructor will speak slowly and clearly 50% of the time, as conversation breakdowns may occur frequently, but not all of the time. The other 50% of the time, the instructor will either whisper or speak the words extremely quickly. Club members will use a coloring page to record any problems that occur as they listen to the instructor's example.

Materials

- "Did Something Go Wrong?" Cards, pages 1–5 (cut out in advance)
- "Did Something Go Wrong?" Part 1 Coloring Page
- Crayon for each club member
- Unit 5 Reinforcement Page

Set-up

Instructor gives each club member a "'Did Something Go Wrong?' Part 1" Coloring Page and a crayon.

Activity Rules

1. Instructor reads one sentence in the manner indicated by the picture clue in the corner.
2. Club member identifies if there was a problem.
3. If a problem occurred, the club member shades the appropriate part of the picture — ears, thought bubble, or box at the bottom — based on the origin of the problem.

Talking Points for Instructor:

"I am going to read you a sentence. If I use a voice that is too quiet, you might not hear my words. If that happens, color in a box under the ear to show that you did not hear me. If I talk too quickly, you might not understand me. If that happens, color in a box under the thought bubble to show that you did not understand me. If I speak in a 'just-right' voice, you will understand me. If that happens, color a box at the bottom to show that you heard and understood my message. The goal is to figure out if there is a problem, and what the problem is!"

Club Agenda

1. Have club members recite the password.
2. Review: Who is Fix It Farrah? What does Fix It Farrah want us to do? Have you ever had a time when someone didn't hear you in a conversation? What did you do?
3. Reread "Let's Fix The Problem" (optional).
4. Introduce activity.
5. Play game.
6. Add club members' points.
7. Wrap up.

Language to Support Learning

"That's right! When I whisper, it is hard to hear what I say."

"You colored a box under the thought bubble. That tells me that you did not understand what I said."

96 | Conversation Club

Activity 3: "Did Something Go Wrong?" Game Part 2

Summary

The focus of this game is for club members to identify when someone else does not hear or understand the conversation. During this activity, one club member will read a sentence from a "Did Something Go Wrong?" Card. Each card also contains a symbol (e.g., a quiet sign in the top corner). If a problem occurs when the club member reads the card, the instructor will make a very obvious facial expression (accompanied by any necessary nonverbal cues) to indicate what the problem was. For example, if the instructor makes an unmistakably confused face and scratches his head, these nonverbal cues tell the club members that the instructor did not understand. If a club member does not recognize or understand nonverbal cues for the feeling of "confused," provide them with the visual representation supplied with this unit as visual support. The second club member will use the instructor's facial expression and other nonverbal cues (if any) to determine if a problem was caused by not paying attention, not hearing, or not understanding. The second club member will check a box below the eyes, ears, or thought bubble to show understanding of where the problem occurred. If there was no problem, he will shade in a box at the bottom.

Materials

- "Did Something Go Wrong?" Cards (cut out in advance)
- "Did Something Go Wrong?" Part 2 Coloring Page
- Crayon for each club member
- Unit 5 Reinforcement Page

Set-up

Instructor gives each club member a "'Did Something Go Wrong?' Part 2" coloring page and a crayon.

Activity Rules

1. Club Member 1 draws or is given a "Did Something Go Wrong?" Card containing one sentence and one symbol. The symbol indicates how the sentence should be spoken. For example, if there is a quiet symbol, they should whisper the sentence. Club Member 1 reads the sentence out loud to the instructor.

2. The instructor then makes a very obvious facial/nonverbal expression to clarify the problem (in this example, she would not hear, so she might turn her head with her ear facing the speaker and lean her head toward the speaker, or cup her ear with her hand).

3. Club Member 2 identifies whether a problem occurred and what the problem was.

4. Club Member 2 shades the eyes, ears, thought bubble, or box at the bottom to reflect whether a problem occurred and, if so, what the problem was.

5. Club members will earn points for "checking in" with their eyes, active listening, checking the box of the appropriate problem, and stating the problem.

Talking Points for Instructor:

"Fix It Farrah has a new challenge for you today! We are going to play the same game as last time. But this time, you will take turns reading sentences to me. I might hear you and understand you, but I might not. After one person reads the sentence, the other person will look at my face to see if I was looking and paying attention. But there could be a different problem. If you say it too quietly, I might not hear you. And if I make a confused face, like this (model), then I might not have understood you. Remember, if you speak in a 'just-right' voice, I should be able to understand your message. The person watching my face should color in a box under the eyes, ears, thought bubble, or bottom, depending on how the conversation went. The goal is to figure out if there is a problem, and what the problem is!"

Club Agenda

1. Have club members recite the password.
2. Review: Who is your favorite Conversation Club character? What is one way Fix It Farrah taught us to fix our conversation? Why does Fix It Farrah want us to notice if our partner is not paying attention?
3. Reread "Let's Fix The Problem" (optional).
4. Introduce activity.
5. Play game.
6. Add club members' points.
7. Wrap up.

Language to Support Learning

"That's right! When you whispered, I could not hear what you said."

"You colored a box under the thought bubble to show that I didn't understand."

"You colored in a box under the eyes because I was not looking when Johnny was talking. That shows I was not paying attention."

Activity 4: "Something Went Wrong. What Do I Do Now?" Game

Summary

This activity is designed to introduce strategies to repair a conversation breakdown. Club members will learn tools from Fix It Farrah's toolbox that they can use if any of the problems from previous activities occur. Tools for each situation are listed under the eyes, ears, or thought bubble, with boxes next to each tool. In this activity, the instructor will model the selection and use of a tool. If the tool worked, the instructor will put a check mark in the box. If the tool did not work, the instructor will put an "X" in the box. When club members are ready, the instructor will take on a facilitation role. Club members will pick up a conversation card with the same picture clues as Activities 2 and 3 (e.g., picture of a quiet sign). If a breakdown occurs, they will again determine why, find the corresponding picture (e.g., eyes, ears, or thought bubble), select a tool, and try using the tool. If the tool works for this situation, club members will mark a box with a check; if not, they will mark an "X" instead.

Materials

- "Did Something Go Wrong?" Cards (cut ahead of time)
- Fix It Farrah's Tools Flow Chart
- "Something Went Wrong. What Do I Do Now?" Coloring Page
- Crayon for each club member
- Unit 5 Reinforcement Page

Set-up

Instructor gives club members the "Something Went Wrong. What Do I Do Now?" coloring page. Instructor will select a "Did Something Go Wrong?" Card and read that message aloud. The instructor will then model how to select a tool, use that tool, and analyze whether or not the tool worked. Next, the instructor takes on a facilitator role. In this scenario, one club member will have the coloring page and the other club member will have the "Did Something Go Wrong?" Cards.

Activity Rules

1. Player 1 picks up one card containing one sentence and one symbol. The symbol indicates how the sentence should be spoken. For example, if there is a quiet symbol, he should whisper the sentence. Player 1 then reads the sentence out loud to the instructor.

2. The instructor will listen to Player 1 read the sentence. If there was a problem (in this example, he would not hear the sentence), the instructor will make a very obvious facial expression showing that there was a problem; he did not hear the message.

3. Player 2 is instructed to look at the instructor's eyes, eyebrows, body language, and facial expression. She will then determine if a problem occurred and specify the reason for the problem (i.e., spoken too softly, so she did not hear).

4. After determining what the problem was, Player 2 will then shade the image of either the eyes, ears, or thought bubble at the bottom of the page. If a problem did not occur, she will shade the box indicating understanding.

5. Club members will earn points for "checking in" with their eyes, active listening, accurately shading the problem, and stating the problem.

Unit 5: Conversation Repair | 99

Talking Points for Instructor:

"Today, Fix It Farrah is going to teach us what to do if a problem happens during conversation. Just like last time, I am going to read sentences, and you will figure out if something went wrong. But this time, under each body part, there are Fix It Farrah's favorite tools. I will try to use one of those tools. If it works, I will put a check mark in the box next to that tool. If it does not work, I will put an 'X' in the box next to that tool. Then you will have a turn using each tool and deciding if it worked."

Club Agenda

1. Have club members recite the password.
2. Review: What is one problem that might happen during a conversation? How would you know if your partner is listening to you? Why is it important to use a "just-right" voice? What would you tell your partner to do if their voice was too quiet?
3. Reread "Let's Fix the Problem" (optional).
4. Introduce activity.
5. Play game.
6. Add club members' points.
7. Wrap up.

Language to Support Learning

"Saying it again did not work because she was still not looking. What could we do instead?"

"Saying your name worked, because I got your attention."

100 | Conversation Club

Activity 5: Fixing Problems in the Moment Activity

Summary

In this activity, club members are introduced to a flow chart to systematically solve problems in the moment. Club members will use the Conversation Tracker introduced to them in Unit 4, Activity 2 to engage in a turn-taking conversation. During the conversation, the instructor will make comments that are too quiet or confusing, or the instructor will purposefully not respond. The club members will then use the flow chart to first determine "was it me or you," identify the problem, and select a strategy to use to repair the breakdown. As the club members become more independent with identifying when problems occur, the instructor should ensure that when a club member uses a strategy, it does not always work. For example, if the club member decides to say it again louder, the instructor may pretend to still not hear them. This promotes flexibility in thinking and problem solving. Club members will get extra points for trying another strategy if one does not work the first time. After the club members have had ample time to use the flow chart with the instructor, the instructor should remove himself from the conversation. Now the club members will have opportunities to repair breakdowns in their own conversations, which is the ultimate goal. Instructors should facilitate this process as needed.

Materials

- Conversation Tracker (Key Words with Conversation Chart from Unit 4, Activity 2)
- Fix It Farrah's Tools Flow Chart
- Unit 5 Reinforcement Page

Set-up

Instructor gives club members a flow chart to use for problem solving conversation breakdowns as they arise and places conversation tracker on the table.

Activity Rules

1. Instructor facilitates conversation using the conversation tracker.
2. Instructor intentionally speaks too quietly, talks very quickly, or attempts to speak when one club member is not paying attention.
3. Club members identify that something went wrong.
4. Instructor facilitates the conversation, using the flow chart to identify and solve the problems.
5. If the tool used did not work, the instructor models using flexible problem solving to select a different tool.
6. When the club members are ready to move on, the instructor removes herself from the conversation, and club members take on both roles.
7. Club members earn points for identifying if there was a problem, stating the problem, identifying a tool, accurately determining if the tool worked to fix the problem, and demonstrating flexibility by selecting an alternate tool.

Talking Points for Instructor:

"Today, we are going to use Fix It Farrah's favorite tools to help us fix problems in a conversation. We are going to ask questions and make comments using a conversation tracker. We are going to look out for times when something goes wrong during our conversation. Remember – that might be if you do not hear the words, do not understand the words, or were not paying attention. Each time something goes wrong, we will stop talking and use Fix It Farrah's chart to help us pick a tool to use!"

Club Agenda

1. Have club members recite the password.
2. Review: What is one problem that might happen during a conversation? How would you know if your partner is listening to you? Why is it important to use a "just-right" voice? What would you tell your partner to do if their voice was too quiet?
3. Reread "Let's Fix the Problem" (optional).
4. Introduce activity.
5. Play game.
6. Add club members' points.
7. Wrap up.

Language to Support Learning

"Repeating what you said is a great tool to use when your friend did not hear you."

"Wow! You used a different tool when saying their name did not work."

"It looked like saying it louder helped Bobby to hear your entire message."

Activity 6: "Are You Interested or Not?" Activity

Summary

Conversation breakdowns may occur for reasons other than misunderstanding, attention difficulties, or missing information. Even if club members are listening to one another, a common cause of conversation breakdowns is that the conversation partner is not interested in the topic at hand. This activity will focus on teaching club members to identify when their partners are not interested in what they are talking about. They will also use various strategies to solve these types of problems. The purpose of this activity is to teach club members to assess their partners' nonverbal cues to determine if they are interested. If the partner is not interested, the speaker should select a tool to use. These tools include asking a conversation partner if he wants to keep talking about that topic, asking what he wants to talk about, or selecting a new topic. Club members will participate in a game in which they will have a stack of Topic Cards. Half of the Topic Cards consist of topics of interest based on their conversation files. The other half of the Topic Cards contain boring topics or topics the instructor knows are non-preferred. The club members will take turns selecting a topic and using the Conversation Tracker for spontaneous conversation. When they hear the predetermined sound selected at the beginning of the session, they must do the "interested or not" check in. During this check in, they will use a visual aid to assess if their conversation partners are interested. If so, they will then continue discussing that same topic. If they are unsure, they will ask their partners if they like the topic or not. If the partners are uninterested, club members will change the topic by selecting a new card.

Materials

- Conversation Tracker (Key Words with Conversation Tracker from Unit 4, Activity 2)
- "Are You Interested or Not?" Topic Cards
- "Are You Interested or Not?" Visual Aid
- Computer or alarm

Set-up

Instructor gives club members a pile of Topic Cards and the Conversation Tracker. Instructor will introduce the "Are You Interested or Not?" Visual Aid during check-in's.

Activity Rules

1. Club members each select a card.
2. Instructor facilitates conversation using the Conversation Tracker.
3. Instructor makes or plays an agreed-upon sound, letting the club members know they should pause the conversation.
4. Instructor models "check-in" procedure, then prompts club members to stop and "check in" to see if their partners are interested in the topic or conversation. Instructors should use the "Are You Interested or Not" visual to help club members interpret nonverbal cues when identifying whether their partners are interested or not.
5. If the club member states that her partner is not interested, she should choose a new Topic Card.
6. Club members earn points for stopping the conversation after hearing the sound, identifying if their partners are interested, changing topics if their partners are disinterested, and asking and answering questions based on the topic.

Talking Points for Instructor:

"Fix It Farrah has another challenge for you today! You are going to have conversations about lots of topics today. Some of the topics are interesting, but some of the topics are really boring. When you pick a topic card, we will use the conversation tracker to talk about that topic. Then, you will hear this sound (play sound). When you hear this special sound, stop talking and 'check in' to see if your partner is interested or not. We will use this worksheet to help us find out if your partner is interested. If he is interested, keep talking! If not, throw away the boring card, and we will pick a new Topic Card to talk about!"

Club Agenda

1. Have club members recite the password.
2. Review: What is one problem that might happen during a conversation? Why is it important to use a "just-right" voice?
3. What tool could you use to fix the problem of not understanding the message? What would you say to fix the problem if your partner was talking too quickly?
4. Reread "Let's Fix the Problem" (optional).
5. Introduce activity.
6. Play game.
7. Add club members' points.
8. Wrap up.

Language to Support Learning

"Asking if they want to talk about something different is a great tool to fix the problem."

"Wow! You both asked so many questions and made so many comments, because you were both interested in the baseball game topic."

Generalization Opportunities

During other times of the day, vary your speech for a couple of sentences by whispering, speaking too fast, mumbling, etc. See if students can use one of Fix It Farrah's strategies (e.g., asking you to repeat it, asking you to say it louder). If they do use a strategy, praise them for *thinking like Fix It Farrah.*

If a breakdown in communication occurs in literature you are reading or a movie you are watching, pause to reflect on why the breakdown occurred and how the club members might fix it.

Reinforce students when they use one of Fix It Farrah's strategies during the school day.

Create a visual with conversation strategies that students can reference during the school day.

If club members are having a difficult time with one or more goals, you might want to consider:

- Repeating an activity
- Modifying an existing activity
- Staging role plays where students can take turns practicing using one of Fix It Farrah's strategies
- Using videos to illustrate a breakdown in conversation, and having students identify when the breakdown occurred and how they might fix it
- Role playing using previously taught methods for gaining attention, such as tapping on the person's shoulder or calling his name for club members who are having difficulty getting someone's attention

Materials

**Unit 5, Activities 2, 3 & 4 Materials:
"Did Something Go Wrong?" Cards Page 1 of 5**

Whispering Voice: Friendly Freddy went to see a movie this weekend.	**Whispering Voice:** Good Memory Maria likes to play at the park.
Whispering Voice: I am feeling very hungry right now.	**Whispering Voice:** I am excited for the weekend.
Whispering Voice: A dog was running outside.	**Whispering Voice:** It is fun having conversations at lunch.

Purchasers of *Conversation Club* are granted permission to print materials from the *Instructor Manual* and *Storybooks* at www.aapcpublishing.net/ccdw. None of the handouts may be reproduced to generate revenue for any program or individual. Unauthorized use beyond this privilege is prosecutable under federal law.

**Unit 5, Activities 2, 3 & 4 Materials:
"Did Something Go Wrong?" Cards Page 2 of 5**

Whispering Voice: It is so sunny at the beach.	**Whispering Voice:** The kids were playing soccer outside.
Whispering Voice: I wonder if it will snow a lot this winter.	**Whispering Voice:** What are you going to eat for dinner?
Just-Right Voice: There are swings and slides at the park.	**Just-Right Voice:** What school do you go to?

Unit 5: Conversation Repair | 107

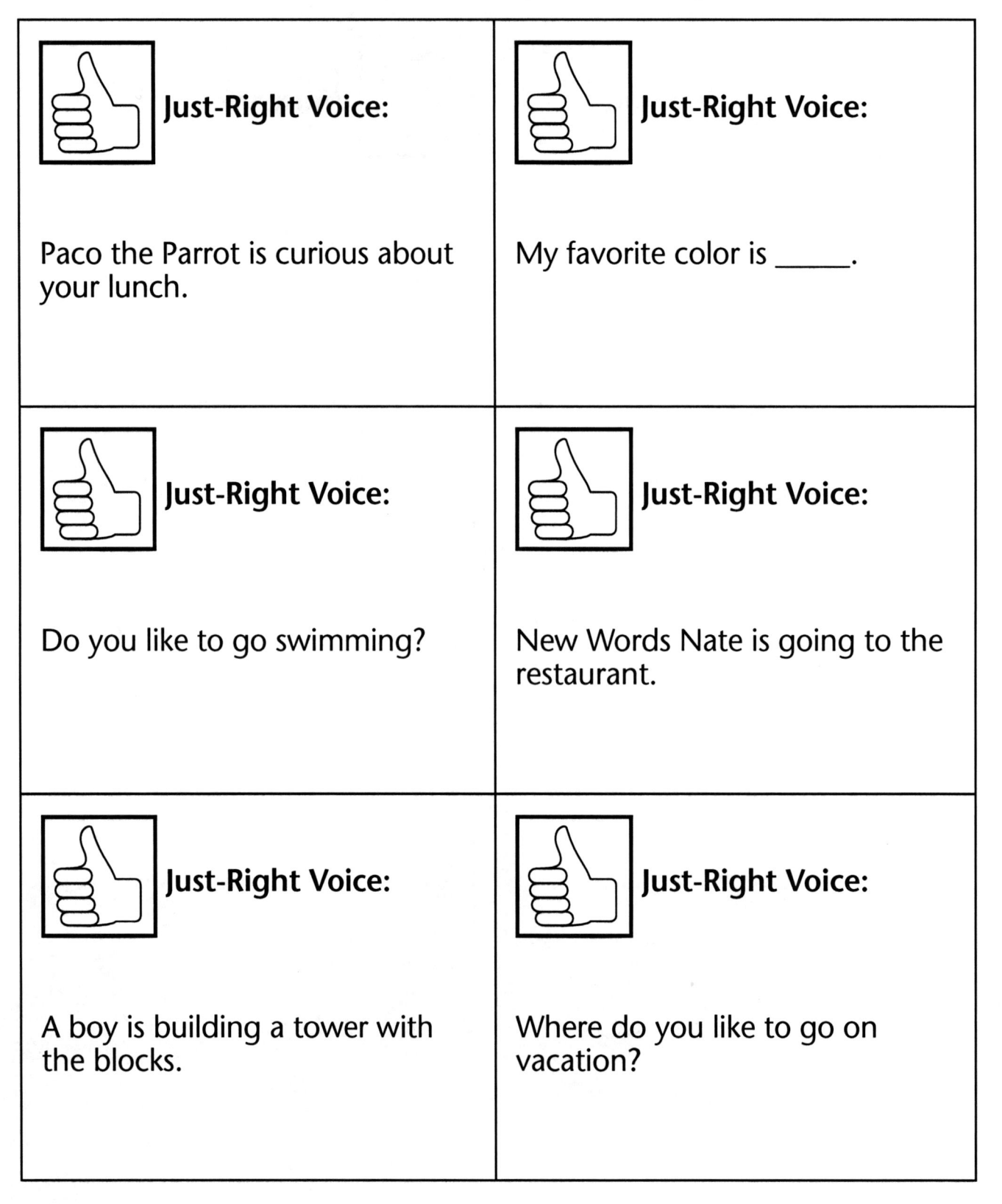

Unit 5, Activities 2, 3 & 4 Materials: "Did Something Go Wrong?" Cards Page 3 of 5

Just-Right Voice: Paco the Parrot is curious about your lunch.	**Just-Right Voice:** My favorite color is _____.
Just-Right Voice: Do you like to go swimming?	**Just-Right Voice:** New Words Nate is going to the restaurant.
Just-Right Voice: A boy is building a tower with the blocks.	**Just-Right Voice:** Where do you like to go on vacation?

108 | Conversation Club

**Unit 5, Activities 2, 3 & 4 Materials:
"Did Something Go Wrong?" Cards Page 4 of 5**

Just-Right Voice: I like traveling on airplanes.	Just-Right Voice: I played a game last weekend.
Too-Fast Voice: I am going to read a story tonight.	Too-Fast Voice: What is your favorite book?
Too-Fast Voice: Did you see the drawing I made?	Too-Fast Voice: This store is so busy.

Unit 5: Conversation Repair | 109

**Unit 5, Activities 2, 3 & 4 Materials:
"Did Something Go Wrong?" Cards Page 5 of 5**

⏩ Too-Fast Voice: I ate pizza for dinner last night.	⏩ Too-Fast Voice: I went to a baseball game.
⏩ Too-Fast Voice: I like to play sports after school.	⏩ Too-Fast Voice: I am hoping it is sunny outside this weekend.
⏩ Too-Fast Voice: I am going to watch TV when I get home.	⏩ Too-Fast Voice: Where do you live?

Unit 5, Activity 3 Materials:
"Did Something Go Wrong?" Part 1 Coloring Page

Did Something Go Wrong?

Did Not Understand

Did Not Hear

Heard + Understood ✓

Unit 5: Conversation Repair | 111

Unit 5, Activity 3 Materials:
"Did Something Go Wrong?" Part 2 Coloring Page

Did Something Go Wrong?

Part 2

Did Not Understand

Did Not Hear

Was Not Looking at Me

Heard + **Understood** ✓

112 | Conversation Club

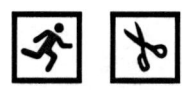

**Unit 5, Activity 4 Materials:
Fix It Farrah's Tools Flow Chart**

Something Went Wrong! ➡ What Do I Do Now?

Did Not Hear TOOLBOX

1. Say partner's name first
   ☐☐☐
2. Say it again
   ☐☐☐
3. Say it louder
   ☐☐☐

Was Not Looking TOOLBOX

1. Say partner's name first
   ☐☐☐
2. Tap partner's shoulder
   ☐☐☐

Did Not Understand TOOLBOX

1. Say it slowly
   ☐☐☐
2. Use different/fewer words
   ☐☐☐
3. Show pictures
   ☐☐☐

Unit 5: Conversation Repair | 113

Unit 5, Activity 5 Materials: Fixing Problems in the Moment Flow Chart

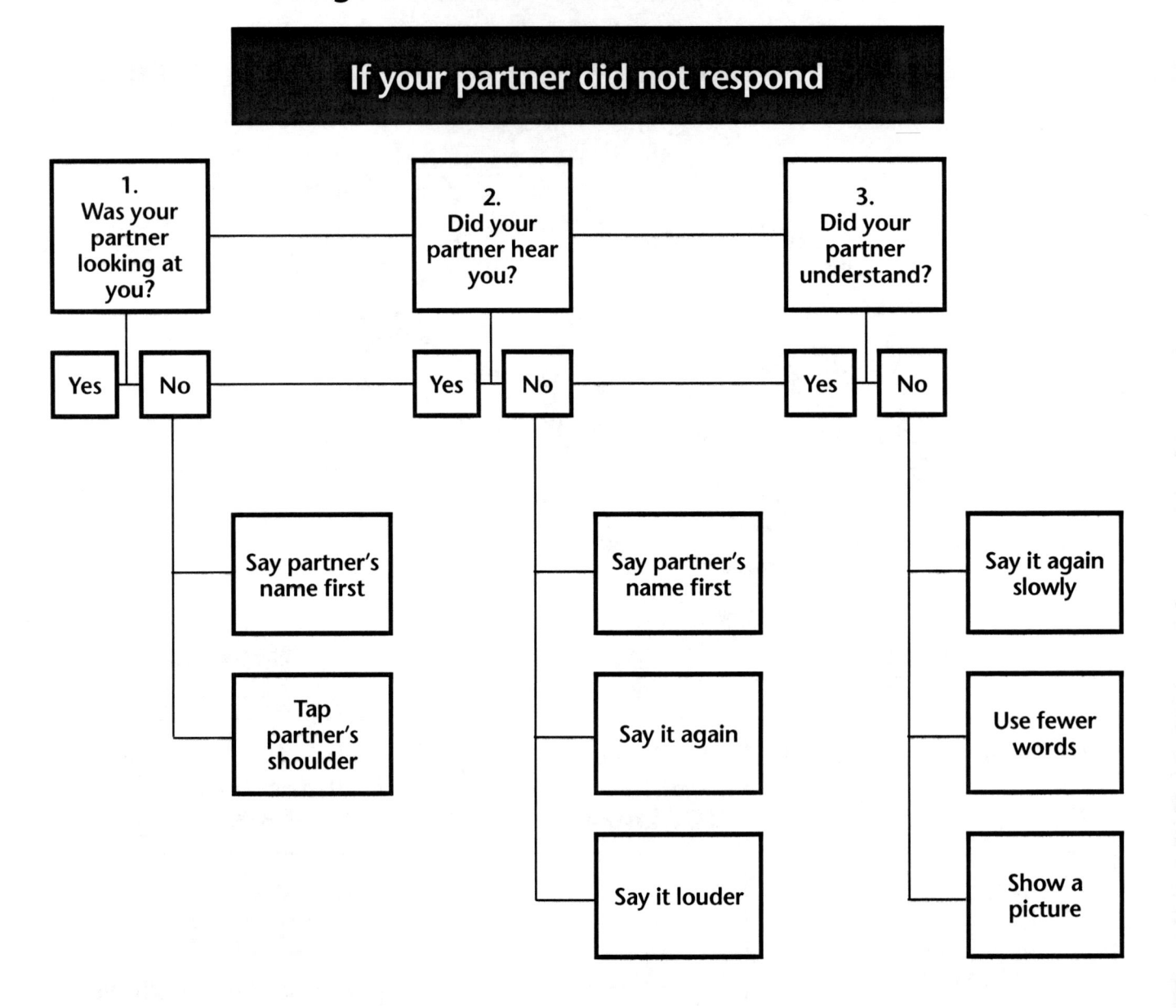

If your partner did not respond

1. Was your partner looking at you?
- Yes
- No →
  - Say partner's name first
  - Tap partner's shoulder

2. Did your partner hear you?
- Yes
- No →
  - Say partner's name first
  - Say it again
  - Say it louder

3. Did your partner understand?
- Yes
- No →
  - Say it again slowly
  - Use fewer words
  - Show a picture

114 | Conversation Club

Unit 5, Activity 6 Materials:
"Are You Interested or Not?" Topic Cards Page 1 of 2

Interesting Topic Cards

Instructor Directions: Write preferred topics based on club members' interests (See Conversation Club Files)

TOPIC	TOPIC
TOPIC	TOPIC
TOPIC	TOPIC

Unit 5, Activity 6 Materials:
"Are You Interested or Not?" Topic Cards Page 2 of 2

Boring Topic Cards

Instructor Directions: Write non-preferred topics based on club members' interests.

_____ _____ **TOPIC**	_____ _____ **TOPIC**
_____ _____ **TOPIC**	_____ _____ **TOPIC**
_____ _____ **TOPIC**	_____ _____ **TOPIC**

Unit 5, Activity 6 Materials: "Are You Interested or Not?" Visual Aid

Unit 5: Conversation Repair | 117

Unit 5: Reinforcement Page

Name:	Name:	Name:
Gain Attention	Gain Attention	Gain Attention
"Check in" with Eyes	"Check in" with Eyes	"Check in" with Eyes
Answer Questions ?	Answer Questions ?	Answer Questions ?
Ask *WH* Questions	Ask *WH* Questions	Ask *WH* Questions

118 | Conversation Club

Unit 6:
Remembering What Our Conversation Partner Says

What Will Club Members Learn?

In this unit, club members will be introduced to Good Memory Maria. She helps club members think about the information shared by their conversation partners, remember it, recall topics that were of interest to their partners, and use the preferred topics in future conversations. Good Memory Maria helps us take the information that was shared and create a mental picture to help us commit this information to memory.

Why Do We Teach This?

The core goals of this unit are to actively listen to our conversation partners and remember what they say. A key strategy for gaining information about peers is to use the active listening strategies presented by Listening Lisa and Looking Louie, such as finding the key words in the statement and "checking in" with our eyes. It is important to show our conversation partners that we remember the information shared during conversation. This is proof that we are interested in the conversation. Children with language processing deficits often have difficulty comprehending, remembering, and utilizing previously learned information. By using active listening strategies, visualization techniques, and other visual supports, club members can use previously learned information to initiate and sustain future conversations with their conversation partners.

Outcome Objectives

This unit teaches club members to do the following:

- Use strategies to improve memory and recall
- Create a mental picture of a statement made during a conversation
- Choose a topic of mutual interest
- Recall who, what, where, or when following a conversation
- Identify whether or not a conversation partner is paying attention
- Use attention-gaining behaviors to gain a conversation partner's attention (e.g., saying partner's name, tapping partner on the shoulder)

Reinforcement

Provide one point each time club members:

- "Check in" with their eyes
- Gain conversation partner's attention
- Ask on-topic *WH* questions

- Answer on-topic questions
- Remember information shared by conversation partner

Activity List

1. *Storybooks:* "Remember What Is Shared"
2. Movement Memory Game
3. Recall *WH* Word Sort
4. Mental Pictionary Game
5. Topic Card Venn Diagram

Activities

Activity 1: "Remember What Is Shared" Story

Summary

The purpose of the story is to introduce club members to Good Memory Maria. Feel free to reread this story as you move through the lessons in Unit 6. In "Remember What Is Shared," club members will observe Good Memory Maria having conversations with other characters. Sometimes she doesn't remember what her conversation partner says. Good Memory Maria demonstrates different ways to improve conversation memory, such as "checking in" with our eyes, remembering key words, and making a mental picture of what our conversation partners say. She also teaches us that remembering information about our conversation partners shows them that we are interested in sharing and learning information about them so they will want to keep hanging out with us.

Materials

- *Storybooks:* "Remember What Is Shared"
- Unit 6 Reinforcement Page

Talking Points for Instructor:

"Today is a big day! We are going to meet the next member of the Conversation Club. She's going to teach us a new club rule and new ways to earn points. We are going to meet Good Memory Maria. She helps us remember what we learned during conversations with our friends. Looking Louie and Listening Lisa will still help us be good listeners so we know what other club members are talking about. When we are good listeners, others will want to be around us and spend more time with us. You will earn points for listening, 'checking in' with your eyes, and answering questions during the story."

Club Agenda

1. Have club members recite the password.
2. Review: What are the names of the Conversation Club characters we have met so far? How do you show club members you are listening to them? What is one reason we have conversations?
3. Read "Remember What Is Shared."
4. Add club members' points.
5. Wrap up.

Language to Support Learning

"Wow, I can tell you were paying attention since you remembered one of Good Memory Maria's tricks!"

"Good Memory Maria would be so proud that you were able to remember information about your conversation partner!"

Unit 6: Remembering What Our Conversation Partner Says

Activity 2: Movement Memory Game

Summary

The goal of this game is to introduce the idea of remembering and recalling information in a short time span. By using their eyes to "check in" with their conversation partners, club members will get information they need to recall and perform.

Materials

- Movement Memory Cards, Pages 1–4 (cut out in advance)
- Unit 6 Reinforcement Page

Set-up

Club members sit or stand in a circle. Instructor places a pile of Movement Memory Cards in the middle of the circle.

Activity Rules

1. Player 1 selects a card from the pile and completes the action or says the word out loud.
2. Player 2 selects a card from the pile and completes the action or says the word out loud.
3. Player 3 selects a card from the pile and completes the action or says the word out loud.
4. Player 4 must do or say the three movements/words in order, based on what she observed and remembered from watching the other players.
5. Players 1, 2, and/or 3 repeat movement/word sequence if needed.
6. Repeat until all players have had a chance to complete the memory challenge.

Talking Points for Instructor:

"Remember meeting Good Memory Maria? She wants to help us remember the information that we hear when we have conversations with our friends. When we remember information about other club members, it shows them we were paying attention and that we care about what they have to say! You will earn a point for each movement or word that you remember. Make sure the movements or words are in the right order!"

Club Agenda

1. Have club members recite the password.
2. Review: Why does Friendly Freddy want us to have conversations? What are Paco the Parrot's favorite words? How do you get club members' attention?
3. Reread "Remember What Is Shared" (optional).
4. Introduce activity.
5. Play game.
6. Add club members' points.
7. Wrap up.

Language to Support Learning

"I could tell you were paying attention to each player and remembered what they shared. Great job!"

"Good Memory Maria would be proud that you were able to remember all of that information."

122 | Conversation Club

Activity 3: Recall *WH* Word Sort

Summary

This activity helps club members practice identifying the key words in a statement (introduced in Unit 4) and gives members practice sorting them into categories. The activity will help club members store information in an organized way for greater recall and retrieval of information.

Materials

- Silly Sentences (cut ahead of time)
- *WH* Word Sort Sheet
- Unit 6 Reinforcement Page

Set-up

Instructor places a pile of silly sentence strips and the *WH* Word Sort Sheet on the table.

Activity Rules

1. Player 1 picks up a silly sentence strip and reads it out loud.
2. Player 2 identifies the key words and sorts them into *who, what, where,* and *when* (*WH*) categories.
3. Player 2 asks a follow-up question to fill in the missing information.
4. Reverse roles and repeat.
5. At the end of the activity, ask each player a memory question related to the topic discussed.

   *If the sequence is too easy for the players, have the club members identify a topic to discuss and complete the *WH* Word Sort Sheet.

Talking Points for Instructor:

"Good Memory Maria has a helpful way for us to remember information. She wants us to listen to what our partner says, then think about who it is about, what they are doing, where they are, and when it happened. We will use a 'who, what, where, when' chart to keep track of everything you learn when you listen to your friend. You will earn a point on the conversation tracker sheet each time you learn something new and add it onto the chart." (NOTE: If a club member says, "I was with my Mom," instructor writes, "Mom" in the WHO category.)

Club Agenda

1. Have club members recite the password.
2. Review: What does Friendly Freddy want us to do? Why does Looking Louie want us to "check in" with our eyes? Why is it important to remember information about the other club members?
3. Reread "Remember What Is Shared" (optional).
4. Introduce activity.
5. Do activity.
6. Add club members' points.
7. Wrap up.

Language to Support Learning

"Wow, using Paco the Parrot's favorite words helped you to remember where Sally went for vacation."

"I could tell you were really listening because you looked at the club members and you remembered all of the information they shared."

Activity 4: Mental Pictionary Game

Summary

This activity is designed to challenge club members to listen and use the key words they hear to create an image in their minds of what their conversation partners are saying. Initially, the instructor will support this process by drawing the scenario on a white board to show club members how to visualize words by turning them into a picture. Using these "mind pictures," club members will be asked to recall the information discussed.

Materials

- Silly Sentences (cut ahead of time)
- White board and dry erase markers
- Unit 6 Reinforcement Page

Set-up

Instructor prepares the white board and markers, and places a pile of the Silly Sentence strips on the table.

Activity Rules

1. Instructor demonstrates visualization by reading a silly sentence strip out loud, identifying the key words, and drawing a scene on the white board to assist with visualization.
2. Player 1 selects a silly sentence strip and reads it out loud.
3. Player 2 identifies the key words.
4. Instructor or one of the players draws a scene based on the identified key words.
5. Reverse roles and repeat.
6. After club members have each had a turn to ask questions about the silly sentences, challenge them to recall the information. Highlight that when club members recall information, it is because they used their listening strategies and made a mental picture.

Talking Points for Instructor:

"Good Memory Maria has a brand new challenge for us. She wants you to remember information by drawing a picture in your mind using the key words that you hear. You will earn a point each time you identify a key word to help make a picture of the silly sentence."

Club Agenda

1. Have club members recite the password.
2. Review: What is a conversation? Where should your body be during conversation? Can you remember one thing you had a conversation about today?
3. Reread "Remember What Is Shared" (optional).
4. Introduce activity.
5. Play game.
6. Add club members' points.
7. Wrap up.

Language to Support Learning

"Awesome job making a mental picture! I could tell it helped you remember the information."

124 | Conversation Club

Activity 5: Topic Card Venn Diagram

Summary

This activity will help club members identify topics that are of interest to themselves, as well as topics of interest to their conversation partners. When the Venn diagram is complete, it will provide a visual of the shared topics that each club member enjoys talking about.

Materials

- Topic Cards (from Unit 2, Activity 4)
- White board or laminated Venn diagram
- Dry erase markers
- Conversation Club Files (from Unit 2, Activity 6)
- Unit 6 Reinforcement Page

Set-up

Instructor provides a Venn diagram visual and places a pile of the Topic Cards on the table.

Activity Rules

1. Player 1 picks up a Topic Card, turns to Player 2, and asks, "Do you like to talk about _____?"
2. Player 2 answers "yes" or "no."
3. Reverse roles and repeat.
4. At the end of the activity, ask each player to identify a topic that they both like to talk about (anything in the overlapping portion of the chart).

Talking Points for Instructor:

"Good Memory Maria has tricks to help us remember what we learn when we are having conversations, but we can also look at the Conversation Club files we made before. Let's find out what topics we each like to talk about, and see if there are things we both like to talk about. You will earn a point each time you add information to the double circle chart. You earn a bonus point if you remember how your conversation partner feels about the topic."

Club Agenda

1. Have club members recite the password.
2. Review: What are Paco the Parrot's favorite words? How do we let other people know we are listening? Why do we have conversations?
3. Reread "Remember What Is Shared" (optional).
4. Introduce activity.
5. Do activity.
6. Add club members' points.
7. Wrap up.

Language to Support Learning

"Great job looking at the Conversation Club file to see if Lynn likes to talk about Sponge Bob!"
"Good Memory Maria would be happy that you remembered that you and Eve like to talk about Cub Scouts!"
"Michal, it looks like you are really thinking about what Kavon said. Are you making a mental picture?"

Unit 6: Remembering What Our Conversation Partner Says | 125

Generalization Opportunities

Throughout the day, highlight when club members are hanging out and talking about topics of shared interest: *"Great job remembering that you both like to talk about football."*

Praise club members when they ask follow-up questions: *"Gwen knows you remember information about her because you asked a follow-up question about her pet snake."*

Promote and highlight when club members remember and recall information about each other: *"You remembered that Jalen had a soccer game yesterday. Nice job asking him about it!*

During content classes (e.g., language arts, read aloud, social studies), help club members create pictures in their minds of what they are hearing. Ask questions like, *"What do you hear? What do you see?"* When club members are asked to recall information, encourage them to go back to the picture in their mind.

If club members are having a difficult time with one or more goals, you might want to consider:

- Repeating an activity

- Modifying an existing activity

- Creating additional visualization opportunities throughout the school day or during group sessions. Start with smaller bits of information (e.g., ask them to close their eyes and describe a familiar object or ask them to close their eyes as you describe an object). For club members who have difficulty creating mental pictures, reinforce the idea that your words are creating an image or "thought picture".

Materials

Unit 6, Activity 2 Materials:
Movement Memory Cards Page 1 of 4

Clap hands once	Clap hands twice
Spin in a circle	Jump up and down
Walk around your chair	Hop on one foot
Touch both ears	Tap your nose
Tap one knee	Tap both knees
Touch one foot	Touch both feet

Purchasers of *Conversation Club* are granted permission to print materials from the *Instructor Manual* and *Storybooks* at www.aapcpublishing.net/ccdw. None of the handouts may be reproduced to generate revenue for any program or individual. Unauthorized use beyond this privilege is prosecutable under federal law.

Unit 6, Activity 2 Materials: Movement Memory Cards Page 2 of 4

Touch one shoulder	Touch both shoulders
Make a circle with your arm	Touch the floor
Stomp one foot	Stomp both feet
Fly like an airplane	Run in place
Laugh out loud	Smile
Frown	Shake your head

Unit 6, Activity 2 Materials:
Movement Memory Cards Page 3 of 4

Say *purple*	Say *blue*
Say *twelve*	Say *ten*
Say *chicken*	Say *frog*
Say *lion*	Say *cat*
Say *dog*	Say *duck*
Say *baseball*	Say *football*

**Unit 6, Activity 2 Materials:
Movement Memory Cards Page 4 of 4**

Say *marker*	Say *paint*
Say *desk*	Say *chair*
Say *dancing*	Say *slide*
Say *book*	Say *movie*
Say *beach*	Say *lake*
Say *cloud*	Say *sun*

130 | Conversation Club

Unit 6, Activities 3 & 4 Materials: Silly Sentences

Suzie ran into the library to find the tiger.
In the car, Drew took a book out of his pocket.
Steve's blue hair was bright in the sun.
The playground was covered in giant ants.
Simon was wearing polka dot pants to school.
Marcy has a mouse sitting on her shoulder.
My sister jumped into a pumpkin.
The dog bakes cookies at home.
The dolphin rode a bike to the beach.
My brother pulled hot dogs out of the sink.
Stephen jumped over a big yellow tree.
The mouse ate a clock.
The cat was wearing a green hat to dinner.
Lindsey skipped in the hallway with a rainbow.
Sean wore a blue snake on top of his head.
The furry spoon was flying out of the backpack.
Alec rode a dinosaur to school.

Unit 6, Activity 3:
WH **Word Sort Sheet**

WHO	WHAT	WHERE	WHEN

**Unit 6, Activity 5:
Venn Diagram**

Same and Different

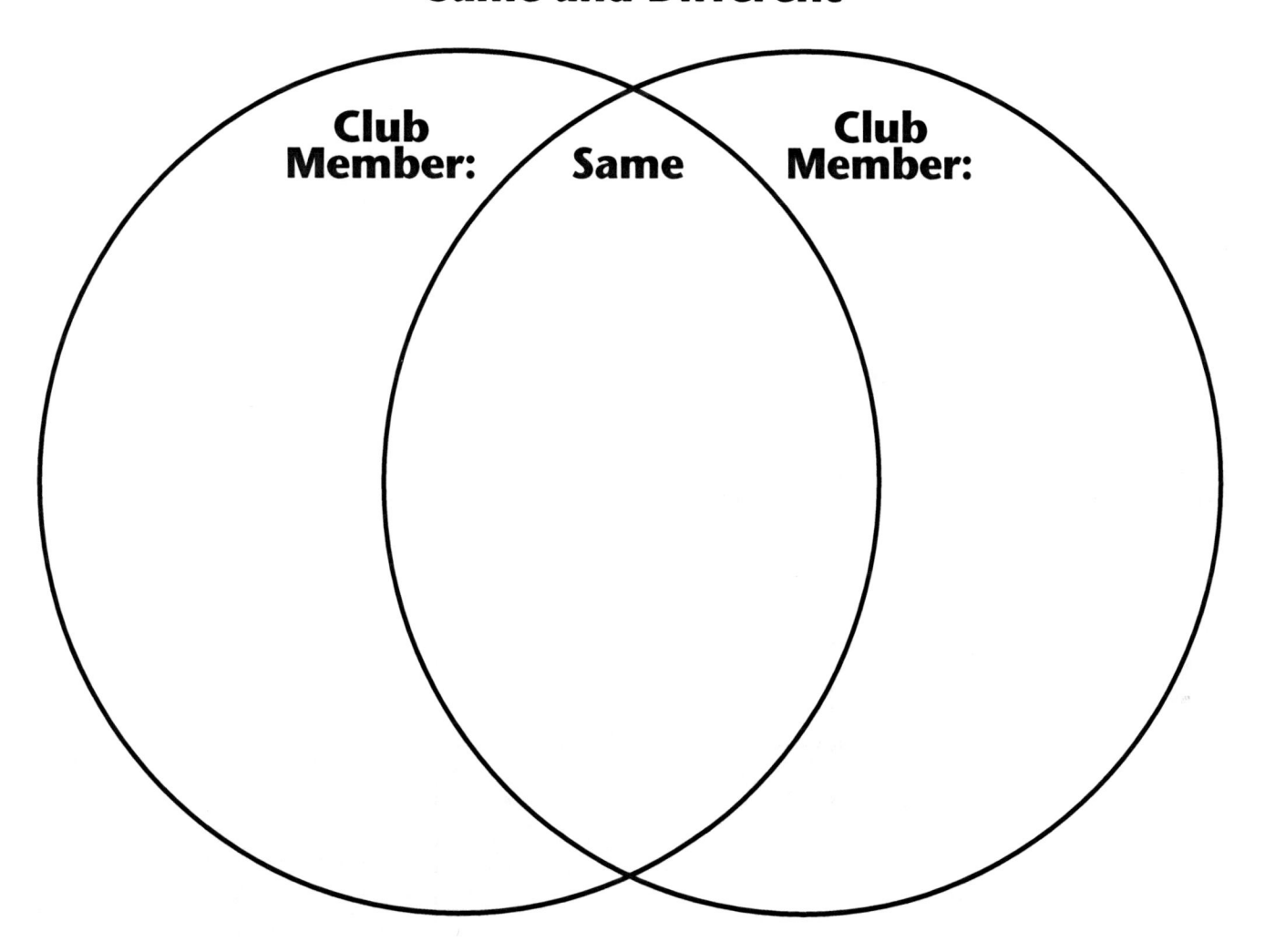

Club Member:

Same

Club Member:

Unit 6: Remembering What Our Conversation Partner Says | 133

Unit 6: Reinforcement Page

Name:	Name:	Name:
Gain Attention 📣	Gain Attention 📣	Gain Attention 📣
"Check in" with Eyes 👀	"Check in" with Eyes 👀	"Check in" with Eyes 👀
Answer Questions ?	Answer Questions ?	Answer Questions ?
Ask *WH* Questions 💬	Ask *WH* Questions 💬	Ask *WH* Questions 💬
Memory 💭	Memory 💭	Memory 💭

Unit 7:
Expanding the Depth and Breadth of Conversation

What Will Club Members Learn?

Club members will be introduced to New Words Nate. He helps club members expand the number and type of question words they use to initiate conversations or keep them going (e.g., *can, would, are,* and *do*). New Words Nate helps club members use previously learned active listening tools to show that they are interested in the information being shared by using friendly words to acknowledge their partners' contributions (e.g., *Neat!, Oh!,* and *Wow!*). Lastly, as conversation naturally shifts from topic to topic, New Words Nate teaches club members to effectively change topics by using a bridging statement (e.g., "That makes me think of…" or "That reminds me of a time when…").

Why Do We Teach This?

This unit focuses on expanding the depth and breadth of conversation in order to facilitate more natural conversational flow. By learning additional question words, club members will have a larger repertoire of words to use when initiating conversation with their partners. However, New Words Nate's job involves even more: he helps remind club members of previously learned strategies, such as finding the key word (introduced by Listening Lisa) and recalling key words (introduced by Good Memory Maria). New Words Nate also helps club members identify when their conversation partners have said something that interests them. If they have heard something interesting, New Words Nate teaches them to use an acknowledging word such as, *wow* or *neat*. By using a friendly, acknowledging word, club members prove not only that they are listening, but that they are interested in the topic at hand and in their conversation partners. Up to this point in the curriculum, conversation has focused on talking about one topic at a time. However, conversation between any two people naturally shifts from topic to topic as information becomes relevant to recent events, past experiences, or personal preferences in an individual's life. In order to facilitate this, New Words Nate teaches club members to topic shift by using a bridging statement. We use thought bubbles and visual aids to demonstrate that when we hear a bridging statement, we should be ready to picture a new topic in our mind. This tool will help club members follow the conversation as it changes from topic to topic, organize the conversation, see that one conversation may be about many different topics, and understand that partners can go back to a topic already discussed. These new strategies introduced by New Words Nate equip club members with more tools to sustain conversations in a natural and organized way.

Outcome Objectives

This unit teaches club members to do the following:

- Use a variety of new question words (e.g., *can, will*) to initiate and sustain conversation
- Use previously learned active listening strategies to determine if they thought the information heard during the conversation was interesting
- Produce an acknowledging phrase (e.g., *Wow!*) after hearing a comment or story they find interesting
- Change a topic smoothly or naturally
- Use a bridging statement when shifting topics (e.g., "That makes me think of…")
- Recall more than one topic that was introduced during the conversation

Reinforcement

Provide one point each time club members:

- "Check in" with their eyes
- Gain conversation partner's attention
- Ask on-topic *WH* questions
- Answer on-topic questions
- Remember information shared by conversation partner

Activity List

1. *Storybooks:* "Let the Conversation Go On and On"
2. New Words Nate Three-Part Question Challenge
3. Friendly Comments Game
4. Repeat *WH* Key Words Activity with New Words Nate's Favorite Words
5. Bridging Topics

Activities

Activity 1: "Let the Conversation Go On and On" Story

Summary

The purpose of the story is to introduce club members to New Words Nate. Feel free to reread this story as you move through the lessons in Unit 7. In this story, club members will join New Words Nate as he celebrates his birthday. New Words Nate will introduce new question words, phrases, and topic shifts. He will demonstrate how club members can use language to keep the conversation going.

Materials

- *Storybooks:* "Let the Conversation Go On and On"
- Unit 7 Reinforcement Page

Talking Points for Instructor:

"Get excited for today! It is time to meet the sixth member of the Conversation Club: New Words Nate! He's going to teach us a new club rule and new ways to earn points. He helps us use more words during conversations with our friends. Looking Louie and Listening Lisa will still help us be good listeners, so we know what other club members are talking about, and so others will want to be around us and spend more time with us. Good Memory Maria will still help us remember what we heard, too."

Club Agenda

1. Have club members recite the password.
2. Review: What are the names of the Conversation Club characters we have met so far? How do you show club members you are listening to them? What is one reason we have conversations?
3. Read "Let the Conversation Go On and On."
4. Add club members' points.
5. Wrap up.

Language to Support Learning

"Wow, I can tell you were paying attention because you just used one of New Words Nate's favorite words!"

"New Words Nate would be so proud that you said, 'Wow!' to show you were interested in what you just heard."

Unit 7: Expanding the Depth and Breadth of Conversation | 137

Activity 2: New Words Nate Three-Part Question Challenge Summary

Summary

The goal of this game is for club members to generate as many questions as they can using New Words Nate's favorite question words (e.g., *could, would, are, did,* and *do*). Club members will play several rounds, earning one point for each question they come up with in each round. Feel free to spread the three-part challenge over multiple days.

Materials

- White board or piece of paper
- Unit 7 Reinforcement Page

Set-up

Club members sit at a table.

Activity Rules

1. Tell club members that today they have a brand new challenge: to come up with as many questions using New Words Nate's favorite words as they can. Club members will earn one point for each question they think of (there will be several rounds). Select a number you think they can achieve (10, 20, or 30).

2. Write down a preferred topic and lay it on the desk (e.g., recess, weekend). Ask club members to think of as many questions about this topic as they can. Keep track of their questions with points. For example, you would provide four points for these questions: *"How was your weekend? Can you run up the slide backwards? Do you like the swings? Did you have fun this weekend?"*

3. Write three or four topics at the top of the board. Ask club members to think of as many questions as they can about these topics. Continue to keep track with points.

4. Add Friendly Freddy's favorite *WH* words to New Words Nate's words for club members to use to make questions. Keep track of questions with points. Add up all of the points at the end to see if the club members reached their goal.

Conversation Club

Talking Points for Instructor:

"Remember meeting New Words Nate? He wants us to use his favorite question words: could, would, did, do, and are. We use these words just like Friendly Freddy's favorite WH words. We use them to ask questions to show that we are thinking about what our friends are saying. This shows our friends that we are interested and helps keep the conversation going!"

Club Agenda

1. Have club members recite the password.
2. Review: What are New Word Nate's favorite words? What question can you ask with New Words Nate's favorite word, *would*?
3. Reread "Let the Conversation Go On and On" (optional).
4. Introduce activity.
5. Play game.
6. Add club members' points.
7. Wrap up.

Language to Support Learning

"That was one of New Words Nate's favorite words!"

"Great job asking a question with New Words Nate's favorite word."

Activity 3: Friendly Comments Game

Summary

This activity is designed to challenge club members to listen to silly/interesting and boring scenarios, then make a mental picture of the scenario. They will practice selecting and using one of New Words Nate's friendly comments, but only if they feel it is interesting. The use of these acknowledging words will show that club members were actively listening and will teach them to use a variety of new phrases to convey interest.

Materials

- Silly and Boring Sentences – Silly/Interesting Sentences (cut ahead of time)
- Silly and Boring Sentences – Boring Sentences (cut ahead of time)
- New Words Nate's Friendly Comment Chart
- White board and dry erase markers (optional)
- Unit 7 Reinforcement Page

Set-up

Instructor places a pile of sentence strips on the table. Instructor has white board and markers.

Activity Rules

1. Instructor demonstrates visualization by reading a sentence out loud. If necessary, the instructor will draw the scene on the white board to assist with visualization.
2. Player 1 selects a sentence strip and reads it out loud.
3. Player 2 creates a picture in her mind of the sentence.
4. Instructor or one of the players draws a scene on the white board based on the identified key words (optional).
5. Player 2 decides if the scenario depicted is boring or silly/interesting. If it is silly or interesting, she uses one of New Words Nate's friendly comments (e.g., *Wow!*).
6. Reverse roles and repeat.

Talking Points for Instructor:

"Today, New Words Nate wants us to listen to sentences and figure out if they are interesting or boring. Some sentences may be funny, silly, or exciting. But some sentences will be really boring. After we read the sentence, we will each make a picture in our mind. Then you will vote for boring or interesting! When we hear something interesting, New Words Nate wants us to use one of his friendly comments such as Wow! or Yeah! to show that we are interested in what our partner said. You will earn a point each time you use one of New Words Nate's comments."

Club Agenda

1. Have club members recite the password.
2. Review: What does New Words Nate want us to do to show that we are listening? Why does New Words Nate want us to use new words?
3. Reread "Let the Conversation Go On and On" (optional).
4. Introduce activity.
5. Do activity.
6. Add club members' points.
7. Wrap up.

Language to Support Learning

"I can tell you were interested because you used one of New Words Nate's friendly comments!"

"New Words Nate would be so proud that you made a picture in your mind for that sentence."

Unit 7: Expanding the Depth and Breadth of Conversation | 141

Activity 4: Repeat *WH* Key Words Activity with New Words Nate's Favorite Words

Summary

This activity is a repeat of the Key Words Conversation Tracker from Unit 4, Activity 2. Using the Conversation Tracker, club members have already learned how to listen for key words and use the Conversation Tracker to record the key words as the conversation progresses. In this activity, they will use the Conversation Tracker to track their conversation, but New Words Nate's favorite question words will also be added to the chart. This will give club members practice asking questions using the following words: *could, would, did, do, can* and *are*. They will still receive points for using *WH* question words during this activity as well. Club members will also get reinforcement for using New Words Nate's friendly comments (e.g., *Cool!, Wow!*).

Materials

- Key Word Conversation Tracker
- New Words Nate's Friendly Comment Chart
- Unit 7 Reinforcement Page

Set-up

Instructor has Unit 7, Activity 4: Key Word Conversation Tracker and New Words Nate's Friendly Comments Chart ready for use.

Activity Rules

1. Club member identifies a topic (Topic Cards can also be used in this activity).
2. As club members ask questions about the topic, the instructor writes down the key word used on the chart (e.g., *mall* would be written down if the club member stated, "I went to the *mall*").
3. Whenever club members use *WH* words or New Words Nate's favorite question words, the instructor will check off the question word at the bottom of the chart, indicating that this specific type of question has already been used.
4. Club members will earn points for using New Words Nate's favorite words, displaying active listening behaviors, and using friendly comments.

Talking Points for Instructor:

"Remember New Words Nate's favorite question words? Who can tell me what they are? You're right. They are could, would, did, do, *and* are. *Today, we are going to use Nate's favorite words to have a conversation. Do you remember the chart? We used this to practice asking* WH *questions. Today, we are going to use this again, but this time, we will also use New Words Nate's favorite words. You can also use his friendly comments (like* Wow!*) to show you are interested. You will earn a point each time you use New Words Nate's favorite words to ask a question or make a comment to show you are interested."*

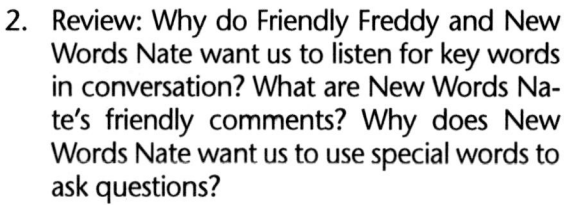

Club Agenda

1. Have club members recite the password.
2. Review: Why do Friendly Freddy and New Words Nate want us to listen for key words in conversation? What are New Words Nate's friendly comments? Why does New Words Nate want us to use special words to ask questions?
3. Reread "Let the Conversation Go On and On" (optional).
4. Introduce activity.
5. Do activity.
6. Add club members' points.
7. Wrap up.

Language to Support Learning

"When you said, 'Cool,' you used one of New Words Nate's friendly comments."

"Great job listening for the key word and then asking a question using one of New Words Nate's favorite question words."

Unit 7: Expanding the Depth and Breadth of Conversation | 143

Activity 5: Bridging Topics

Summary

Club members will learn to use bridging statements when they want to change a topic. A bridging statement that they can insert between two topics may include: "That reminds me of…"; "That makes me think of…"; or, "Oh, yeah, did you know that…?" Club members will participate in three activities using Topic Cards; these will probably require more than one session. Club members will use a bridging sentence visual to help create a picture in their minds of how a bridging sentence helps them move smoothly from one topic to another. They will also receive reinforcement for using Good Memory Maria's recall strategies by going back to a previously discussed topic.

Materials

- Topic Cards (from Unit 5, Activity 6)
- Bridging Sentence Visual
- White board and dry erase markers (optional)
- Timer
- Key Word Conversation Tracker
- Unit 7 Reinforcement Page

Set-up

Instructor places a pile of the topic cards on the table.

Games

1. **Topic Shift**: Each player receives two Topic Cards and a New Words Nate's Bridging Sentence Visual. Players will look at the cards and practice using a bridging statement using key words about each topic. For example, if they have a spring break Topic Card and a vacation Topic Card, they will use a sentence such as, "I wonder if you are going on vacation anywhere for spring break."

2. **Topic Throw Down**: Each player receives five Topic Cards to hold in their hand. The goal of the game is to get rid of all the Topic Cards. The instructor will set the timer for 5 minutes, and Player 1 starts the game by putting down one Topic Card. When the timer goes off, Player 2 will throw down a new Topic Card and must use a bridging sentence to change the topic. The game ends when all the Topic Cards have been used. Throughout the game, the instructor will use the Conversation Tracker to track the conversation as the players move through the Topic Cards.

3. **Topic Bonanza**: The goal of this game is to see how many topics the players can shift between. Using the Conversation Tracker and New Words Nate's Bridging Sentence Visual, players will earn points every time they change a topic. Players can set a goal in the beginning for the number of topics they are aiming for (e.g., 10, 20, or 30 topics). NOTE: Instructors should feel free to spread these activities over multiple days.

Talking Points for Instructor:

"New Words Nate has more to teach us! Most of the time, when we have conversations, we talk about many topics. We might start talking about a topic like gym. Gym might make us think about recess. And recess might make us think about our favorite sports. If we are talking about the weekend and want to change the topic to movies, New Words Nate wants you to use a bridging sentence like, 'That reminds me of the movie I am going to see on Saturday.' You will earn one point each time you use one of New Words Nate's bridging sentences to change a topic."

Club Agenda

1. Have club members recite the password.
2. Review: What are New Words Nate's friendly comments? Why do we use topics during conversation? Why does New Words Nate want you to use new question and comment words?
3. Reread "Let the Conversation Go On and On" (optional).
4. Introduce activity.
5. Do activity.
6. Add club members' points.
7. Wrap up.

Language to Support Learning

"Great job adding a bridging sentence to change the topic!"

"New Words Nate would be so proud that you remembered to add a bridging statement."

Generalization Opportunities

Praise club members when they ask follow-up questions using New Words Nate's question words: *"Ava knows you were paying attention to her because you asked a follow-up question about her trip to the beach."*

Promote and highlight when club members employ active listening skills and use a friendly comment to show that they were interested: *"You just showed Eric that you were interested in his words when you said, 'Yeah!'"*

During the day, highlight when club members are changing topics of shared interest: *"Great job remembering to use a bridging sentence to show that you were changing the topic."*

If club members are having a difficult time with one or more goals, you might want to consider:

- Repeating an activity
- Modifying an existing activity
- Looking ahead to future activities to see if that skill is practiced in other lessons
- Creating additional visualization opportunities throughout the school day or during group sessions

Materials

Unit 7, Activity 3 Materials:
Silly and Boring Sentences Page 1 of 2

Silly/Interesting Sentences

A monkey flew an airplane to the beach.	A snowman is sliding down the hill.
The pool was full of balloons.	The penguin is eating your lunch!
The girl ordered popcorn at the movie theater.	The girl ice skated on the ice skating rink.
The zoo animals are dancing.	The ducks are playing football.
The dog ran after the basketball.	Your teacher is wearing your backpack.
The boy ate a purple pizza for dinner.	The principal is singing into her phone.
The teacher jumped on top of the table.	The little kids are selling lemonade.
A cat played the piano.	A lion wants to give you a high five.
There is an elephant driving that car!	The kids are skipping around the room.

Purchasers of *Conversation Club* are granted permission to print materials from the *Instructor Manual* and *Storybooks* at www.aapcpublishing.net/ccdw. None of the handouts may be reproduced to generate revenue for any program or individual. Unauthorized use beyond this privilege is prosecutable under federal law.

Unit 7, Activity 3 Materials:
Silly and Boring Sentences Page 2 of 2

Boring Sentences

The apple is red.	The teacher is standing.
The tree is tall.	The boy wore shoes.
There is a silver car.	Her shirt is big.
The ice is cold.	The lettuce is green.
The soccer ball is round.	The toy broke.
The boy is sitting.	They have finished eating.
There is a bench.	The water is hot.
There is a dog.	The book is rectangular.
The cat is lying down.	The napkin is clean.

**Unit 7, Activity 3 Materials:
New Words Nate's Friendly Comment Chart**

New Words Nate's
Friendly Comments

Wow Nice Cool Yeah

**Unit 7, Activity 4 Materials:
Key Word Conversation Tracker**

Conversation Tracker

| WHO | WHAT | WHERE | WHEN | CAN WOULD | ARE DO |

150 | Conversation Club

**Unit 7, Activity 5 Materials:
Bridging Sentence Visual**

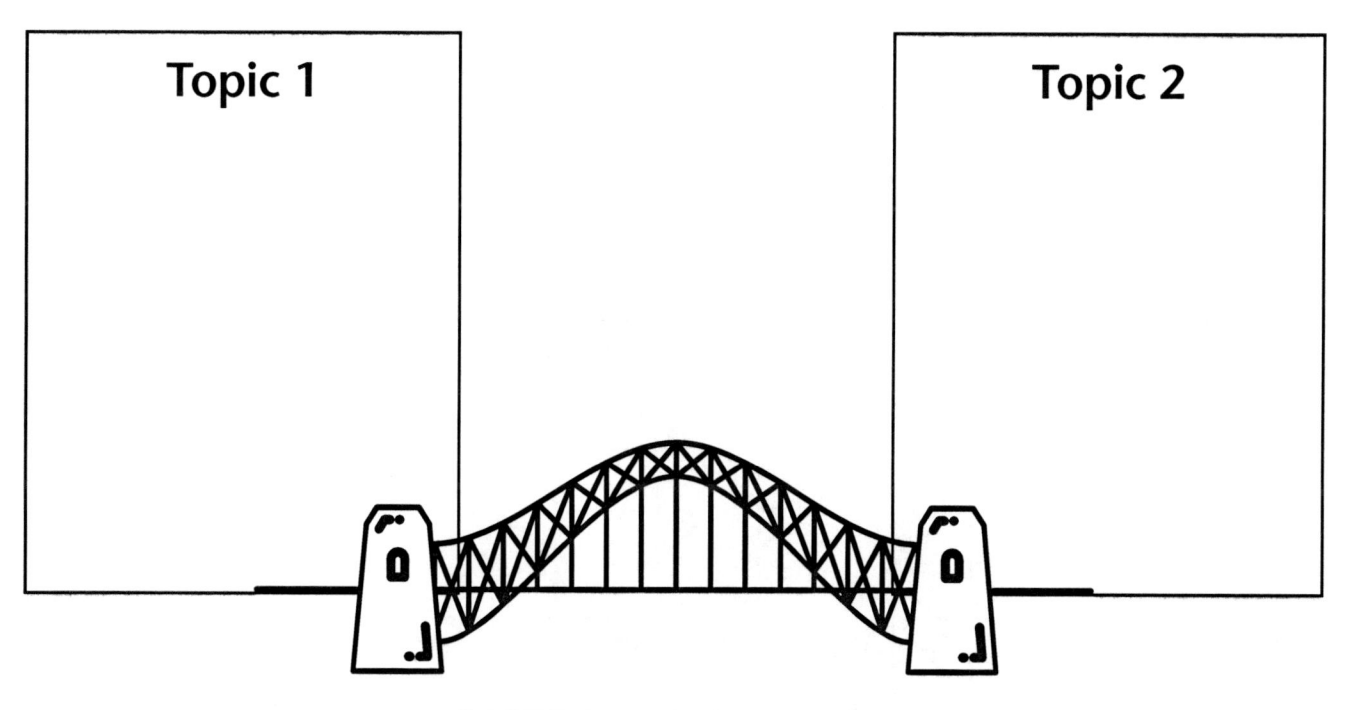

Topic 1

Topic 2

INSERT A SENTENCE:

That reminds me of _____.

That makes me think of a time when _____.

_____ makes me think of _____.

Unit 7: Expanding the Depth and Breadth of Conversation | 151

Unit 7: Reinforcement Page

Name:	Name:	Name:
Gain Attention	Gain Attention	Gain Attention
"Check in" with Eyes	"Check in" with Eyes	"Check in" with Eyes
Answer Questions ?	Answer Questions ?	Answer Questions ?
Ask *WH* Questions	Ask *WH* Questions	Ask *WH* Questions
Memory	Memory	Memory

152 | Conversation Club

Unit 8: Bringing It All Together

What Will Club Members Learn?

In Unit 8, club members will integrate the skills they have learned in Units 1–7. Members will continue to work on making related comments to keep the conversation going and show that they are paying attention to the conversation. Club members will use a clubhouse tree visual to illustrate the progression of their conversation. The branches represent the flow of the conversation from one topic to another. The leaves represent the follow-up comments and details related to a specific topic. Club members will use this visual to help them recall what they have learned about other club members during the conversation. During the final activity of the unit, club members will have the opportunity to share what they have learned in a group review game.

Why Do We Teach This?

The core goals of this unit are to continue helping club members identify and explore the connected and continuing nature of conversations and build a social memory for the information they are learning about their peers. Children with social cognitive deficits often experience quite a bit of anxiety about having conversations with others. Not only are conversations unpredictable, it is hard to know what turns the conversation will take (i.e., *"Will my peer want to talk about what I want to talk about?"*). During conversations, this can be challenging, as the child continually reverts back to their specific area of interest or has difficulty integrating the information their peers add to the conversation. The clubhouse tree visual illustrates the flow of conversation and helps club members visualize and integrate each member's contributions. It is also true that many children with social cognitive deficits have trouble seeing or recalling the "big picture" of an event or conversation. They can easily become bogged down by or hyper-focused on the details. The clubhouse tree visual helps club members to see the conversation with its subtopics and details as components of the larger conversation, or the "big picture." For example, information about Florida, sting rays, sunburns, and getting car sick all relate to the larger topic of vacation. Finally, the clubhouse tree visual helps club members build a social memory for the information their peers have shared and integrate it into a specific context or schema for that individual. These skills are important steps, not only for developing meaningful relationships and integrating newly learned information into their knowledge of a person, but for demystifying the unpredictable nature of conversations.

Outcome Objectives

This unit teaches club members to do the following:

- Propose more than one on-topic follow-up question and/or comment to keep the conversation going.
- Acknowledge and integrate a shift in the topic or subtopics of conversation.
- Recall information from a previous conversation and use it in follow-up conversations.
- Identify a subtopic and make a connecting statement or question to shift the conversation.

✓ Reinforcement

Provide one point each time club members:

- "Check in" with their eyes
- Gain conversation partner's attention
- Ask on-topic *WH* questions
- Answer on-topic questions
- Remember information shared by conversation partner

Activity List

1. *Storybooks:* "Party Time!"
2. Blossoming Trees
3. Conversation Club Collaboration Game

Activities

Activity 1: *Party Time!* Story

Summary

The purpose of the story is to help club members see how all of the skills they have learned throughout the curriculum come together as the club members plan a party to celebrate the Conversation Club. This book is slightly different from the previous books, and club members will be asked to track the different conversation skills they see on display during the course of the story.

Materials

- *Storybooks:* "Party Time!"
- Unit 8 Reinforcement Page (club members will be using this form to track the conversation skills of the characters in the book.)

*To celebrate the culmination of the Conversation Club, it may be fun to have a small celebration with club members. Planning for the celebration could be a great way to practice conversation skills!

Talking Points for Instructor:

"Conversation Club members are planning a party and they need your help. We will have two very important jobs. The first is to be detectives and figure out when club members are using their conversation skills and when they need our help. The second is to help them plan their party!"

Club Agenda

1. Have club members recite the password.
2. Review: What are the names of the Conversation Club characters we have met? Why do we have conversations? How can we show our conversation partners we are interested in what they are saying?
3. Read "Party Time!"
4. Add club members' points.
5. Wrap up.

Language to Support Learning

"Your comment was on-topic. I can tell you were really thinking about what your conversation partner said."

"I can tell that Thomas felt really happy when you listened and made comments about what he said."

Unit 8: Bringing It All Together | 155

Activity 2: Blossoming Trees

Summary

In this lesson, club members will work on keeping the conversation going by building a brainstorm web based on an identified topic. The purpose of the brainstorm is to help club members activate prior knowledge about a topic. After they have completed the brainstorm, club members will start a conversation about that topic. Instructors track the flow of the conversation using the blossoming tree visual. The branches reflect the related topic changes. The leaves on the branches reflect the details related to the topic. To reinforce social memory and the process of thinking about each other, club members will be asked to recall what other club members shared during the conversation.

Materials

- White board
- Piece of paper or Blossoming Tree Supporting Visual (see example on page 161)
- Unit 8 Reinforcement Page

Set-up

Write the topic in the middle of the piece of paper for the super brainstorm. Use a white board to create the outline of the clubhouse tree as club members converse.

Activity Rules

1. Pick a topic that all club members have an interest in (e.g., spring break, football, TV shows). Ask club members to think of as many words as they can related to that topic (e.g., spring break: plane, car, vacation, beach, grandma, relax, fun, no homework). Write these words on the white piece of paper.

2. Prompt club members to start a conversation about the topic. Club members may need support as they attempt to generate questions. If they need support, list Paco's and Nate's favorite words as visual cues (*what, who, where, did you…*, etc.).

3. Track club conversations by recording their topics on a tree visual (see example on page 162). New subtopics should go on the branches; details about that topic should go on the leaves (e.g., spring break: *trunk*; Florida: *branch*; family: *leaf*; hot: *leaf*; snorkeling: *branch*; colorful fish: *leaf*). (*Instructor tip: Do not get hung up on the tree branches and leaves needing to look a certain way. The goal is to have club members see that conversations grow and change, and that by asking questions and making comments, they contribute to the conversation.*)

4. After the conversation, ask club members to state one thing they learned during the conversation. Club members can reference the clubhouse tree visual to support their recall.

5. Club members will earn points for asking questions, answering questions, "checking in" with their eyes, getting each other's attention, and remembering things about each other.

Talking Points for Instructor:

"The whole Conversation Club gang has a goal for us. They want us to have interesting conversations. Friendly Freddy wants us to share lots of information. Paco the Parrot wants us to use his favorite words to find out the details about a topic. Looking Louie and Listening Lisa want us to use our eyes and ears to find out information about what club members are thinking and feeling. Good Memory Maria wants us to remember information about the conversations we have, and New Words Nate hopes we will use his super cool words to keep the conversation going. So let's see if we can put it all together and have some great conversations. You will earn points for asking questions, answering questions, "checking in" with your eyes, getting each other's attention, and remembering things about each other!"

Club Agenda

1. Have club members recite the password.
2. Review: What are New Words Nate's favorite words? When you want to make other club members feel good about what they said, what are some comments you can make? Why would you want to change topics in a conversation?
3. Reread "Party Time!" (optional).
4. Introduce activity.
5. Do activity.
6. Add club members' points.
7. Wrap up.

Language to Support Learning

"Wow, look at our clubhouse tree visual! You can really tell how our conversation about summer vacation changed and grew during our conversation."

"Talking about summer vacation made you think about not having homework, and that is why you changed the conversation to talk about how long your homework takes each night."

"I can tell you were thinking about your friends, and you remember a lot of what they shared during the conversation today."

Activity 3: Conversation Club Collaboration Game

Summary

This board game is designed to help club members review and practice the skills they have learned during the course of the curriculum. Club members will take turns selecting a card, answering a question, and moving around the game board. The object of the game is to have *all* club members reach the Conversation Clubhouse.

Materials

- Conversation Club Collaboration Game Board
- Game Cards, pages 1–3
- Conversation Club Collaboration Game Pieces
- Unit 8 Reinforcement Page

Set-up

Instructor places Game Cards and Game Board on the table.

Activity Rules

1. Remind club members that the goal is for each club member to make it around the Game Board and reach the Conversation Clubhouse.
2. Each club member chooses a Game Piece (club characters).
3. When it is his turn, the player picks a card and reads the question aloud. He must try to answer the question. If he does not know the answer, he can pick a club member to help answer the question.
4. When all characters have made it around the Game Board and up to the tree house, the game is over.
5. Club members will earn points for asking questions, answering questions, "checking in" with their eyes, getting each other's attention, and remembering things about each other.

Talking Points for Instructor:

"Club members, it has been a pleasure to be in the Conversation Club with you. Freddy, Paco, Lisa, Louie, Nate, Maria, and Farrah have taught us so much about conversations. To celebrate our club, we are going to play a game to show how much we have learned. The great thing about this game is that we are all a team. To win this game, all of the club members have to make it back to the tree house. You will earn points for asking questions, answering questions, 'checking in' with your eyes, getting each other's attention, and remembering things about each other."

Club Agenda

1. Have club members recite the password.
2. Review: What is the Conversation Club? Why do we have conversations? Name one thing the Conversation Club members have taught you.
3. Reread "Party Time!" (optional).
4. Introduce game.
5. Play game.
6. Add club members' points.
7. Wrap up.

Language to Support Learning

"I liked the way you got Sam's attention. You said his name and then tapped him on the shoulder."

"Great job working together and having a conversation about the answer."

"I love the friendly comments you used when Juan answered the question."

Unit 8: Bringing It All Together | 159

Generalization Opportunities

Share skills club members are working on and the tips for assisting them with other individuals in their lives (e.g., parents, therapists, teachers). If a prompt, visual aid, or specific support is particularly salient, encourage others to use the same language.

During reading activities, highlight when characters are displaying targeted conversation skills:

"Oh, you could really tell she was thinking about what her friend liked when she started talking about Mario Brothers."

"It does not sound like this conversation is going well. Both people are talking about different topics. What could they do to improve the conversation?"

Time filler: When you find yourself with a couple of extra minutes before or after a class or session, pose questions about Conversation Club:

"What would Friendly Freddy like us to do right now?"

"How would Looking Louie want us to find out more information about the person we are talking to?"

"New Words Nate would definitely have a suggestion for a way to get more information about the picnic."

Write your own Conversation Club adventure. What better way to see what the club members have retained than to ask them to create a story about the Conversation Club characters. Options for adventures the characters can take are endless!

If club members are having a difficult time with one or more goals, you might want to consider:

- Creating a new character to address the unique needs of your club members.

- Repeating a lesson that addresses a specific breakdown the club members need help with.

- Taking a break from the lessons and letting club members chat as you observe their strengths and breakdowns.

Materials

Unit 8, Activity 2 Materials:
Blossoming Trees Supporting Visual Brainstorm Example

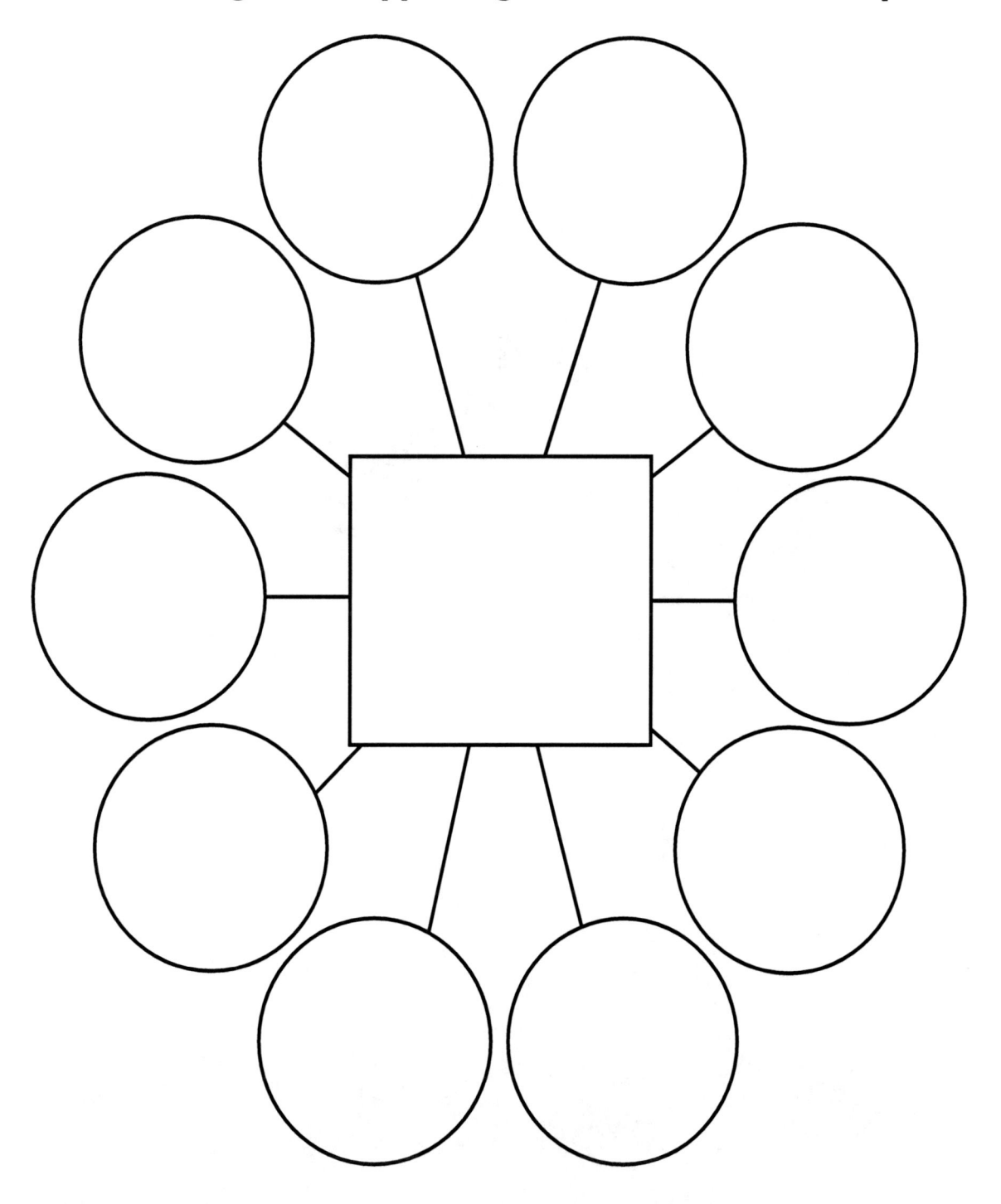

Purchasers of *Conversation Club* are granted permission to print materials from the *Instructor Manual* and *Storybooks* at www.aapcpublishing.net/ccdw. None of the handouts may be reproduced to generate revenue for any program or individual. Unauthorized use beyond this privilege is prosecutable under federal law.

Unit 8: Bringing It All Together | 161

Unit 8, Activity 2 Materials:
Blossoming Trees Supporting Visual Tree Example

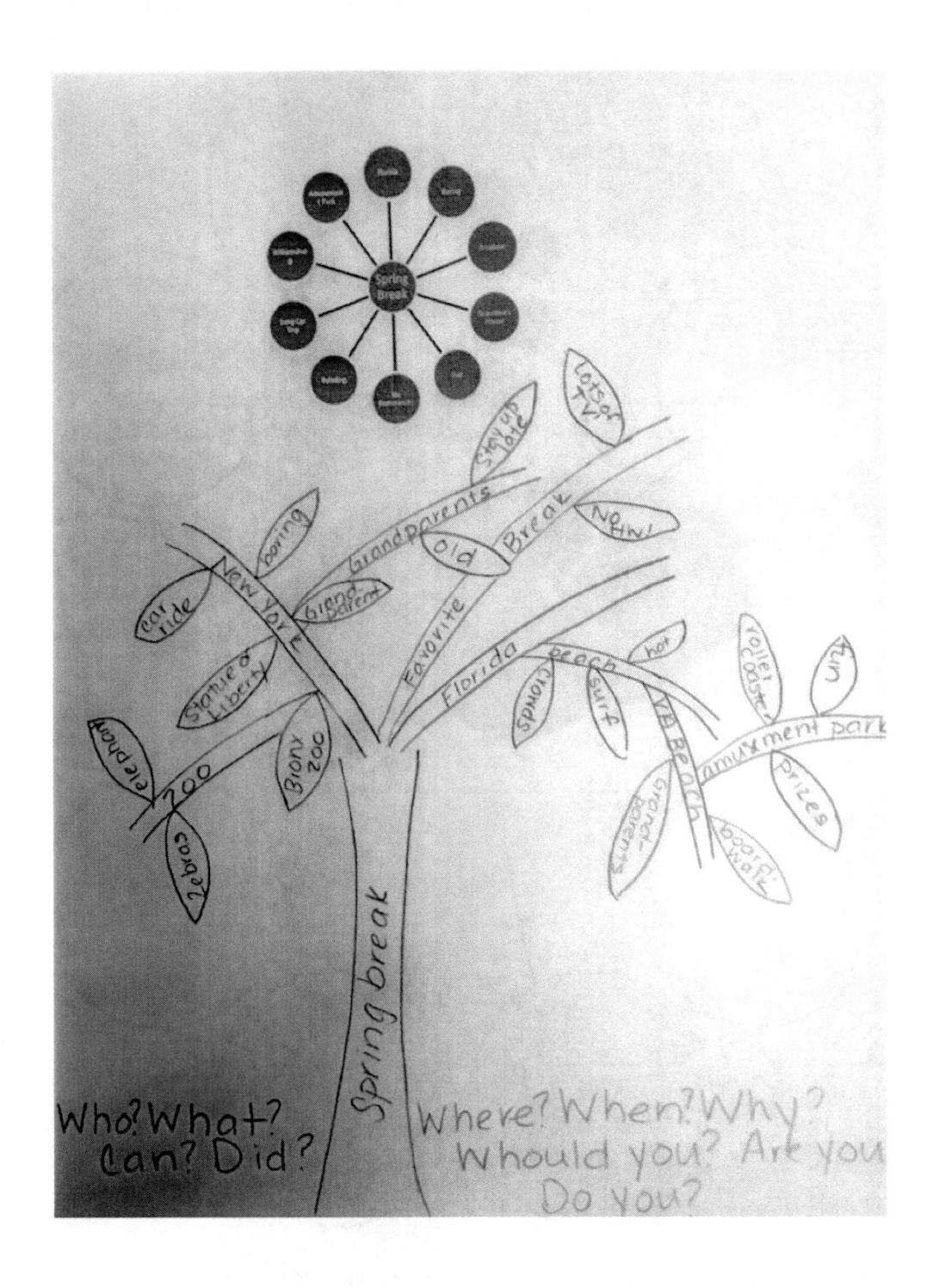

162 | Conversation Club

Unit 8, Activity 3 Materials: Conversation Club Collaboration Game

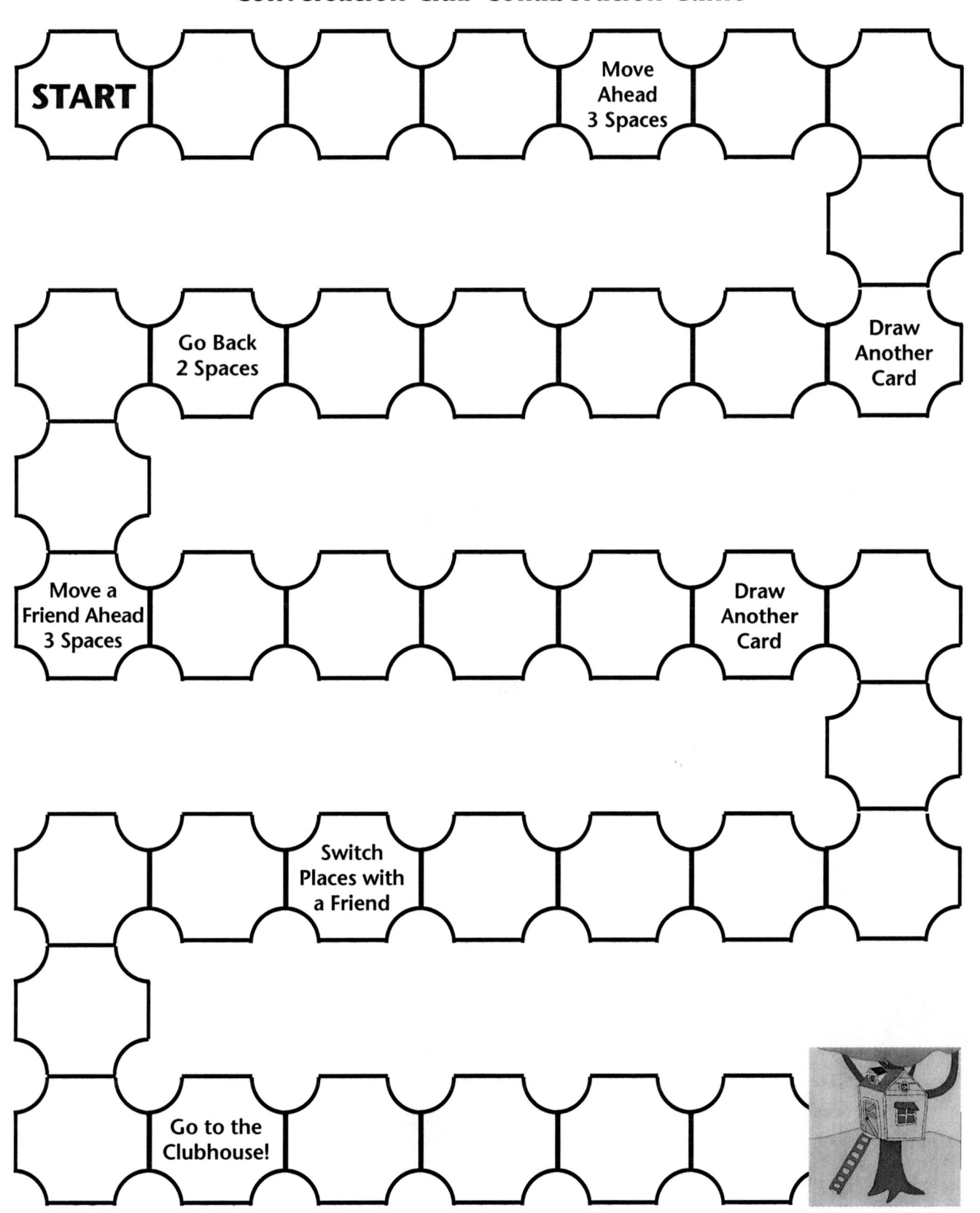

START

Move Ahead 3 Spaces

Draw Another Card

Go Back 2 Spaces

Move a Friend Ahead 3 Spaces

Draw Another Card

Switch Places with a Friend

Go to the Clubhouse!

Unit 8: Bringing It All Together | 163

Unit 8, Activity 3 Materials:
Conversation Club Collaboration Game Pieces

164 | Conversation Club

Unit 8, Activity 3 Materials: Game Cards Page 1 of 3

Conversation Club! Who is the president of the Conversation Club?	Conversation Club! What does Friendly Freddy want us to do?
Conversation Club! Why do we have conversations?	Conversation Club! What is a topic?
Conversation Club! What is your favorite topic to talk about?	Conversation Club! What are Paco the Parrot's favorite words?
Conversation Club! If I want to know what time something happened, what WH words would I use?	Conversation Club! Ms. Wilson went to the beach on Saturday. Do we know when Ms. Wilson went? Do we know where Ms. Wilson went?
Conversation Club! What is one topic you know the person sitting across from you likes?	Conversation Club! Why is it important to select a topic your friend likes?

Unit 8: Bringing It All Together | 165

Unit 8, Activity 3 Materials:
Game Cards Page 2 of 3

Conversation Club! What is your Conversation Club's super, secret password?	**Conversation Club!** Answer this WHEN question. When do you have lunch?
Conversation Club! Answer this WHAT question. What do you have for lunch today?	**Conversation Club!** Answer this WHERE question. Where do you keep your pencil?
Conversation Club! What does Listening Lisa want us to do?	**Conversation Club!** What does Looking Louie want us to do?
Conversation Club! Listen to this statement. What is the key word? What word would you use in your follow-up statement? "I like to play soccer"	**Conversation Club!** Name two strategies you can use to get someone's attention.
Conversation Club! Who helps "fix" a problem we have in our conversation?	**Conversation Club!** How do I know if someone did not hear what I said during our conversation?

Unit 8, Activity 3 Materials:
Game Cards Page 3 of 3

Conversation Club! What happens if our partner is not paying attention during the conversation?	**Conversation Club!** Why does Good Memory Maria want us to remember what our friends say?
Conversation Club! How does your friend feel when you pick a topic they like to talk about?	**Conversation Club!** I am going to say a sentence. "I went on the slide at recess." What do you picture the slide to look like?
Conversation Club! Name two of New Word Nate's favorite words.	**Conversation Club!** Use a bridging statement to connect these two topics. School and Recess
Conversation Club! Name three Conversation Club members.	**Conversation Club!** Who is your favorite Conversation Club member? Why?
Conversation Club! What is your favorite part of Conversation Club?	**Conversation Club!** Name two times during the day that you like to have conversations.

Unit 8: Bringing It All Together | 167

Unit 8: Reinforcement Page

Name:	Name:	Name:
Gain Attention 📣	Gain Attention 📣	Gain Attention 📣
"Check in" with Eyes 👀	"Check in" with Eyes 👀	"Check in" with Eyes 👀
Answer Questions ?	Answer Questions ?	Answer Questions ?
Ask *WH* Questions 💬	Ask *WH* Questions 💬	Ask *WH* Questions 💬
Memory 💭	Memory 💭	Memory 💭

168 | Conversation Club

Unit 8: Certificate of Achievement

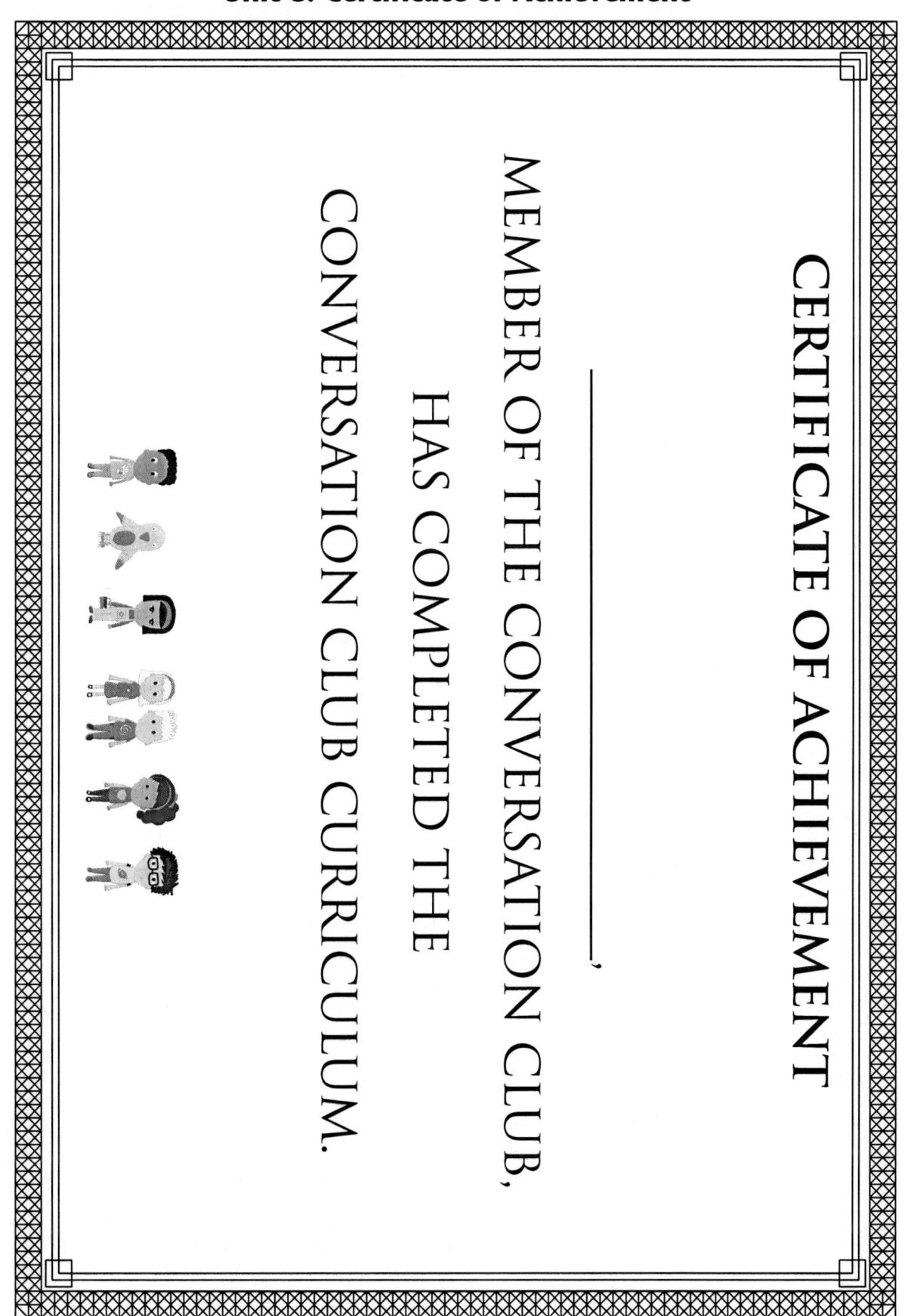

CERTIFICATE OF ACHIEVEMENT

_____,

MEMBER OF THE CONVERSATION CLUB,

HAS COMPLETED THE

CONVERSATION CLUB CURRICULUM.

References

Baron-Cohen, S., Leslie, A., & Frith, U. (1985). Does the autistic child have a "theory of mind"? *Cognition, 21,* 37- 46.

Baron-Cohen, S., Wheelwright, S., Hill, J., Raste, Y., & Plumb, I. (2001). The 'Reading the Mind in the Eyes' Test Revised Version: A study with normal adults, and adults with Asperger Syndrome and high-functioning autism. *Journal of Child Psychology and Psychiatry, 42,* 241-252.

Burack, J., Charman, T., Yirmiya, N., & Zelazo, P. (2001). *The development of autism: Perspectives from theory and research.* Mahwah, NJ: Lawrence Erlbaum Associates.

Dotson, W., Leaf, J., Sheldon, J., & Sherman, J. (2010). Group teaching of conversation skills to adolescents on the autism spectrum. *Research in Autism Spectrum Disorders, 4,* 199-209.

Fiske, S., & Taylor, S. (2013). *Social cognition: From brains to culture* (2nd ed.). Thousand Oaks, CA: SAGE Publications.

Goddard, L., Howlin, P., Dritschel, B., & Patel, T. (2007). Autobiographical memory and social problem solving in Asperger syndrome. *Journal of Autism and Developmental Disorders, 37,* 291-300.

Klin, A., Jones, W., Schultz, R., & Volkmar, F. (2003). The enactive mind, or from actions to cognition: Lessons from autism. *Philosophical Transactions of the Royal Society of London, 358,* 345-360.

Leaf, J., Dotson, W., Oppenheim, M., Sheldon, J., & Sherman, J. (2010). The effectiveness of a group teaching interaction procedure for teaching social skills to young children with a pervasive developmental disorder. *Research in Autism Spectrum Disorders, 4,* 186-198.

Leaf, J. Taubman, M., Bloomfield, S., Palos-Rafuse, L., Leaf, R., McEachin, J., & Oppenheim, M. (2009). Increasing social skills and prosocial behavior for three children diagnosed with autism through the use of a teaching package. *Research in Autism Disorders, 3,* 275-289.

Madrigal, S., & Winner, M. (2009). *Superflex takes on Glassman and the team of Unthinkables.* San Jose, CA: Think Social Publishing.

Müller, E., Cannon, L., Kornblum, C., Clark, J., & Powers, M. (2016). Description and preliminary evaluation of a curriculum for teaching conversation skills to children with high-functioning autism and other social cognition challenges. *Language, Speech and Hearing Services in Schools, 47*(3), 191-208.

Payton, J., Weissberg, R. P., Durlak, J. A., Dymnicki, A. B., Taylor, R. D., Schellinger, K. B., & Pachan, M. (2008). The positive impact of social and emotional learning for kindergarten to eighth-grade students: Findings from three scientific reviews. Technical Report. *Collaborative for Academic, Social, and Emotional Learning (NJ1).*

Striano, T., & Reid, V. (Eds.) (2008). *Social cognition: Development, neuroscience and autism.* Hoboken, NJ: Wiley-Blackwell.

Tanweer, T., Rathbone, C., & Souchay, C. (2009). Autobiographical memory, autonoetic consciousness, and identity in Asperger Syndrome. *Neuropsychologia, 48,* 900-908.

Wetherby, A & Prizant, B. (2000). *Autism spectrum disorders: A transactional perspective.* Baltimore, MD: Paul H. Brookes Publishing Company.

Winner, M. G. (2007). *Social behavior mapping.* San Jose, CA: Think Social Publishing.

Zins, J. E., Bloodworth, M. R., Weissberg, R. P., & Walberg, H. J. (2007). The scientific base linking social and emotional learning to school success. *Journal of Educational and Psychological Consultation, 17*(2-3), 191-210.

About the Authors and Illustrator

Lynn Cannon, MEd, is the Social Learning Coordinator at the Ivymount School. She is responsible for helping develop and oversee the social learning curriculum for the Model Asperger Program, the Multiple Learning Needs Program, and the early childhood program at the Maddux School. In that capacity, she works with teachers and therapists to develop and implement evidence-based social learning curricula. Lynn has a B.A. in psychology and elementary education from the College of William and Mary and a master's degree in special education from the University of Virginia Curry School of Education. Lynn is the Curriculum Coordinator of the Take2 Summer Camp, a program designed to develop interaction skills and social thinking in children ages 8 through 12 in Washington DC. Lynn is the lead author of an NIH-funded intervention, Unstuck and On Target (Brookes Publishing), that targets flexibility and goal-directed behavior in children with autism spectrum disorders and ADHD. Lynn and collaborating authors are currently working on several social learning manuals and research projects, including the *Unstuck and On Target* companion manual for middle school students and *On Target for Life.*

Jonna Clark, MS, OTR/L, earned her Master of Science in occupational therapy from Ithaca College. She served as an occupational therapist at the Ivymount School, where she worked with students ages 5 through 21 with physical, social, and developmental challenges. She honed her collaboration skills and training with other special education professionals to develop a variety of classroom programs. Throughout her time working in schools, she has also worked in private clinics and worked closely with families to develop home programs. Jonna currently works with school-aged children in the public school system near Seattle, WA, helping children with a variety of challenges become more independent and successful in the school setting.

Courtney Kornblum, MA, CCC-SLP, TSSLD, is the department head of the Speech Language Pathology Team at the Parkside School in New York, NY. She provides speech and language therapy to elementary school children who come from diverse ethnic, social, and economic backgrounds and have a range of language-based learning difficulties. Courtney enjoys collaborating with an interdisciplinary team as well as supporting the professional development of the speech and language department. She graduated with honors from the Pennsylvania State University with a Bachelor of Science degree in communication sciences and disorders and a minor in human development and family studies. She received her Master of Arts degree in speech and hearing sciences from the George Washington University. Courtney previously served as a speech language pathologist at the Ivymount School and the Maddux School, primarily working with elementary school children with varied speech and language challenges attributed to autism spectrum disorders, developmental delays, specific learning disabilities, and other health impairments. Thanks to the collaborative and transdisciplinary nature of these programs, Courtney and her colleagues had the opportunity to create and implement the *Conversation Club* curriculum.

Eve Müller, Ph.D., is the Coordinator of Program Evaluation and Outcomes Research at the Ivymount School, where she evaluates the effectiveness of various programs and curricula for students on the autism spectrum. She received her Ph.D. in education and autism spectrum disorders (ASD) from UC Berkeley and has published extensively on ASD and social and emotional learning. She is a co-author of the forthcoming *Ivymount Social Cognition Instructional Package (IvySCIP)*, a comprehensive online program that supports instructors of K–6 students with high-functioning ASD through all phases of social and emotional learning instruction — from assessment through IEP goal development, selection of curricular resources, and progress monitoring. Prior to completing her doctoral work, she managed residential and integrated work programs serving adults with ASD.

Michal Powers, LCSW-C, RPT, has been a practicing clinical social worker since 1997, specializing in therapy with children and adolescents with special needs in residential, out-patient, and school settings. Michal has a B.S. in psychology from the University of Massachusetts at Amherst and a master's degree in social work from the Catholic University of America. Michal has also taught preschool, where she witnessed the important role of play not only for learning but for emotional and social development. This rich experience was the motivation for obtaining a certification as a registered play therapist. Since 2010, Michal has provided mental-health counseling services to elementary- and middle-school children with developmental disabilities in the Ivymount School's Multiple Learning Needs program. In addition to providing individual and small group counseling sessions, Michal facilitates the *Conversation Club* Curriculum.

Bobby Whalen lives in Washington, DC, with his family. He has been drawing, illustrating, and creating magical art, stories, and animations his whole life. He is a high school student at the Ivymount School and has autism. Bobby aspires to be an illustrator for Scholastic Books and plans to live independently and travel.

Ivymount Instructional Resource Series

The Ivymount Instructional Resources Series offers a collection of innovative educational resources — including curricula, assessment tools, and apps — designed and tested by Ivymount staff to support the success of students with autism spectrum disorders and other learning challenges. Products are developed by cross-disciplinary teams of expert Ivymount teachers, related service providers, and program evaluators, and are thoroughly vetted in Ivymount classrooms.

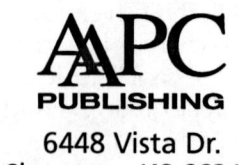

AAPC PUBLISHING

6448 Vista Dr.
Shawnee, KS 66218
www.aapcpublishing.net